# Professional Christian?

# Professional Christian?

## A Cautionary Tale for Pastors and Church Leaders

BILL McCONNELL

TATE PUBLISHING
AND ENTERPRISES, LLC

Published by Tate Publishing & Enterprises, LLC
127 E. Trade Center Terrace | Mustang, Oklahoma 73064 USA
1.888.361.9473 | www.tatepublishing.com

Tate Publishing is committed to excellence in the publishing industry. The company reflects the philosophy established by the founders, based on Psalm 68:11,
*"The Lord gave the word and great was the company of those who published it."*

Book design copyright © 2012 by Tate Publishing, LLC. All rights reserved.
*Cover design by Rtor Maghuyop*
*Interior design by Jake Muelle*

Published in the United States of America

ISBN: 978-1-62147-260-5
1. Religion / Christian Ministry / Pastoral Resources
2. Religion / Christian Ministry / Preaching
12.09.24

# Dedication

To those pastors who labor in supposed anonymity, Jesus knows your labors and is watching.

# Table of Contents


Introduction . . . . . . . . . . . . . . . . . . . . . . . . . . . . . . . . . . . . . . 9

Becoming a Christian . . . . . . . . . . . . . . . . . . . . . . . . . . . . 13

The Baptist Church . . . . . . . . . . . . . . . . . . . . . . . . . . . . . 23

The Other Baptist Church . . . . . . . . . . . . . . . . . . . . . . . 57

The Big Church . . . . . . . . . . . . . . . . . . . . . . . . . . . . . . . . 74

The Reformed Church . . . . . . . . . . . . . . . . . . . . . . . . . 102

The Mega Church . . . . . . . . . . . . . . . . . . . . . . . . . . . . . 119

The Community Church . . . . . . . . . . . . . . . . . . . . . . . 143

The Last Church . . . . . . . . . . . . . . . . . . . . . . . . . . . . . . 156

Conclusion . . . . . . . . . . . . . . . . . . . . . . . . . . . . . . . . . . . 243

Epilogue . . . . . . . . . . . . . . . . . . . . . . . . . . . . . . . . . . . . . 245

# Introduction

One of my favorite movies is *Jeremiah Johnson*. It is the story of a man in the 1830s who tires of life in the city and decides to become a trapper in the Rocky Mountains. His first few weeks are a mixture of farce and adventure as he tries to figure out how to live in this new environment. His ability to survive in the wilderness is in doubt until a grizzled old mountain man teaches him how to live as a trapper and helps him survive. At the end of the movie, after Jeremiah has not only survived but become somewhat of a legend both to the Indians and other mountain men, he stumbles across the old man who had helped him years before. As they sit together around a campfire eating roast rabbit, neither speaks for a time. Then the old mountain man says to Jeremiah, "You have come far, pilgrim." Jeremiah ponders this for a moment and then says, "Feels like far," summing up in three words the totality of his experiences as a mountain man.

I have wandered through the evangelical world in the United States for almost forty-six years, through a number of churches, and I can echo the statement of Jeremiah Johnson, "Feels like far." It is probably a normal experience as we age to try and make sense of what has occupied our lives, and the evangelical church has occupied a large place in my life, both in terms of time and importance. This journey has at times been confusing, uplifting, and disappointing. As a committed follower of Christ, I have never questioned the role of the church in my life, but I have wondered many times what Jesus has thought about the institution that He chose to be His hands and feet in the world.

These are my observations about how going to various churches has impacted me and my family throughout the years. You will discover there are some recurring themes, no doubt because some of the churches I attended had many of the same characteristics and some of the situations that I found myself in had common elements from one church to another. One of the principles that I hope comes across is that churches are shaped by the pastor and those who are leaders; how they minister will determine the effectiveness and success of their churches and in some manner the experience of those who attend. For the most part, I have stayed away from writing about the people who also attended the churches I was involved in. That would be the subject of another book. These are my memories. No doubt some people mentioned in the story will have different recollections about the same event or events. This is normal in life; our memories and observations are colored by our backgrounds, prejudices, and our desire to make ourselves appear in either a good or bad light. Everything that I have written about actually happened, though I do not claim to have remembered every event perfectly. I have wanted to make this as anonymous as possible, so the names of people have been changed. Some of the locations and circumstances have been altered as well; these changes have not affected the story or the characters in the least. Any errors or misstatements are certainly mine alone.

This book was written specifically for pastors and those who are considering going into the ministry. I have included a series of observations written for you that come out of my experiences with these seven churches. No book can ever deal with every subject involved in being a pastor, but I have included some things that will not be found in other books on this subject. These observations are not listed in any order of importance or sequence. I have not dealt with any of these topics at length; my object is to give you things to consider from a different perspective and to help you begin a conversation with other pastors and church leaders on some of these matters. You will also notice that I have not included many references to the Bible. I do not mean this to be a book on church philosophy, structure, or management (though it will touch on these areas); there are many books that deal with those issues from a strictly biblical perspective.

Finally, following these observations or principles are a series of questions to think about in terms of your specific church and ministry. I have found it is profitable on occasion to stop and review, evaluate, and step back from my life to see exactly what is going on and how I might better do the work God has given me. I hope these questions can help you see how you are doing as a pastor and suggest to you different ways you can think about and approach your ministry.

# Becoming a Christian

Orange County, California, was probably the best place to grow up in the United States in the 1960s. Besides having a perfect climate where the sun shone over three hundred days a year, it was prosperous and everything was new—houses, industry, schools, freeways, even Disneyland. My dad worked, as many dads did, for an aerospace firm, a committed member of the middle class, and had designs on moving up the economic ladder, designs that he would eventually realize. His job was quite stressful; he would later describe his job as a middle manager in his company using the classic phrase "rat race." We could have lived in the city closer to his work, and for a time we did. But in the summer of 1968, there were race riots in the city, and we moved to the suburbs within a few months. I can still remember my mom watching these events unfold on the TV and wondering aloud if we would all be caught up in the violence (we weren't). Because he wanted to live in the suburbs (his idea of the American dream included living in the suburbs as opposed to the "city"), a lot of his stress could be attributed to the fact that he had to drive nearly thirty miles on a crowded freeway to work each day, and when he came home, you did not talk to him until he had a chance to take a shower and decompress a bit. He did not like having other people tell him what to do, and he retired as soon as he could get a pension and then went into business for himself as a real-estate broker. My mom worked for a while but then became a housewife. That was more the norm then as now, when it seems that today both the mom and the dad have to work to be financially secure.

I was an only child and found most of my identity though the friends that I made at school. When I was in the seventh grade we moved from one suburb to another, and I entered a new school, eager to make friends. One of the first friends that I made was Steve, a kid who was outgoing, fun, and a natural athlete. Although somewhat heavy, Steve would play football and baseball at the varsity level in high school and become an accomplished golfer and bowler, as well. I was never much of an athlete, but that did not matter to Steve, and we became friends for years to come. His friends became my friends, and I was quickly absorbed into his social orbit. There was one thing about Steve that was new to me: he and his family regularly attended a Baptist church and were faithful Christians. I had at this point in my life never attended church, had no idea what a Christian was, and had never held a Bible in my hands or uttered a prayer.

Because Steve lived close to the school and my home was pretty far away, after school we would go over to his house to hang out. He had a basketball hoop, and we played hours of basketball listening to the radio. I eventually met his parents, stepdad and mom, who were the antitheses of my mom and dad. They were outgoing, seemed genuinely interested in me, and went out of their way to make me feel welcome. I forget how long it took for them to invite me to church, but it eventually happened. I went with Steve to the youth group meeting on Wednesday night and found that these kids were fun to be with, and whatever thoughts I might have had about church (I don't think they were many at that point in my life), they now included the fact that church was fun.

Though I had never attended church before, I was a pretty moral person, even as a kid. I never really did anything wrong (my children reading this might disagree, but of course they did not know me then) and never caused my parents any grief or heartache (they assumed that because I did not cause them any problems that raising children was pretty easy; this would cause dificulty in the years to come). That is not to say that they viewed my going to church with approval; they were pretty much practical atheists who lived to attain the highest standard of living that they could, which they achieved later in life. (This would coincide with the view that Francis Schaeffer, noted Christian philosopher, had of America at this time that the majority of Americans sought personal peace and affluence.)

They never interfered with my new interest in church, a Baptist church no less, and if they had, I do not know what I might have done. When they looked at what was happening in the culture to many kids—getting involved in drugs, protesting the war in Vietnam, having casual sex—they might have looked on my going to church as a blessing (though they probably never would have admitted it). But they didn't interfere, and I became absorbed into this new world, a journey that continues to this day.

One of the abiding mysteries of my relationship with my parents is that, though I tried on a couple of occasions to bring up the subject of Christianity, I was politely but firmly told they were not interested; for over four decades they have expressed no interest in my Christianity, never asked a question, never mentioned anything about church, and only attended one when my children got married.

Evangelicalism is its own subculture and as such has its own vocabulary, practices, values, dress, and other oddities. For a teenager who had never been to church, everything was new, yet I did not experience any type of culture shock or have trouble fitting into this new place. Looking back, I think that the people went out of their way to make me welcome, and like most people, I wanted a place where I felt I belonged. Because my home life left a lot to be desired in terms of acceptance, warmth, and love, I gravitated to the church, where I was accepted, loved, and included in their family. (It is interesting to note that the family metaphor is one of the ways the New Testament describes the church, the term *brother* being used frequently by New Testament writers.) Sometime during that first year of attending church, I became a follower of Jesus. Nobody talked or walked me through how to become a Christian, but after reading the Bible nonstop for that first year (my first Bible was a King James Version my mom bought at Sears, of all places. I came home from youth group one night and announced to her that I needed a Bible, words that I am sure she thought she would never hear from her son); the whole plan of Jesus dying for my sins all made perfect sense.

It still makes perfect sense to me all these years later, though I do not claim to understand everything in the Bible.

During those first few years, I learned the songs and the words and the phrases that belong to evangelicalism. I learned about the service (choir, songs, announcements, sermon, invitation, etc.) and all of those things that make up a typical Sunday morning church experience. This was 1968, and we were right on the edge of the coming revolution in how church would be experienced in the future. Everything in society was changing. It was the year Martin Luther King and Bobby Kennedy were assassinated. The Vietnam War was beginning to be opposed by more and more people, drugs were just finding their way onto high school and college campuses, and the middle-class values that embodied much of the American landscape were being rejected by the children of those who strove to achieve what they thought was the American dream. It was obvious to anyone who was paying attention that the evangelical church was not going to come out of this upheaval unchanged, but few in the church were paying attention. The average church service and indeed the entire structure of the church had not changed in decades and due to its conservative nature would be caught totally unprepared for what was to come, especially in terms of how it ministered to its young people. One of the things that I did not learn about at this time was what went on behind the scenes in the average evangelical church—the power struggles, the gossiping, the dynamic between the board and the pastor. This knowledge would come with time (sometimes I wish it hadn't). I was having too much fun being with the youth group and learning about the Bible to even realize there was anything other than what I was experiencing going on at the church. Like most teenagers, my focus was narrowed to myself, and it wasn't until years later that I was told about what was going on between the pastor and some grown-ups in the church.

Everyone has expectations when they go to church. They have expectations about what they will experience, what they will learn, what they will sing, how their children will feel about church, and how the church will grow. Unfortunately, most of these expectations fall squarely on the shoulders of the pastor, making the job of pastor one of the most difficult in our society. Unlike the business world where people are paid for their work and have a measure of accountability to those who oversee them, churches largely rely on volunteer labor. The pastor has to lead people who have no accountability to him; he must do so with grace, wisdom, and tact. In fact, a church is the exact opposite of what happens in the "real" world. In the real world, you get paid by an employer who has the expectation that you will act in the best interests of the company and follow the procedures and guidelines of the company. Your employer also has a measure of authority over you by the simple fact that he is compensating you for your efforts. In a church, the pastor is paid by the offerings of the people, who many times will not accept his leadership or authority because they are supplying his income.

In our society, it is the one who pays the salary that has the authority and the expectation of accountability, not the other way around as the situation exists in a church. Though the New Testament gives the pastor and other elders authority in church matters, this authority is simply not recognized by most congregations. As a result, the statistics on pastors leaving the ministry are startling; you can Google the phrase "pastor burnout" or "pastor statistics" and find out for yourself (more on this later), but suffice it to say that a majority of pastors quit the ministry in their first five years, and few find any real job satisfaction or sense of purpose in being a pastor. If a pastor can meet the expectations of most of the congregation, then things will by and large go well. If the opposite is true, that for whatever reason he is not meeting the expectations of the church members, be those expectations right or wrong, then there is going to be trouble (of course the pastor can try and change the expectations of the congregation to be in line with his; good luck on that). If those in leadership are among those who are not happy, then the odds are great that the pastor is a goner. That was happening at my church, though I certainly was not aware of it, nor do I think any other young person was aware of the efforts swirling in the background to get rid of the pastor.

# Principles for the Pastor

1.  *Evangelism.* Let's admit right from the beginning that most of the congregation will never be involved in personal evangelism. By this, I mean that they will not either look for opportunities to share their faith or take advantage of opportunities when they arise. There are many reasons for this, but let's dwell on what the pastor can do to get them involved in seeing people come to Christ. While people find it difficult to talk about Christ, there are many people in the church who will invite their family, neighbors, and friends to events if the functions are specifically geared toward reaching these people. These events need to be planned well, promoted for several weeks, and have as the goal to get those who show up to have a good time and see that it is okay to mingle with those who attend evangelical churches. These events should not have any kind of invitation, message, or gospel presentation. What you are aiming for is to eventually get these people to attend the worship service, so it is usually best to hold the event at a location other than the church.

    There are many different types of events to consider. Churches can form an event committee to plan, promote, and organize this type of outreach. There are people in nearly every church who could take this type of ministry and run with it. It may take several of these to get members to invite their friends. Be patient and be sure to encourage those who are leading this ministry. Some pastors prefer to keep throwing different strategies against the wall, as it were, and see what works and what doesn't. Pastors will have to decide for themselves what works for their situation and what kind of programs complement their gifts and the talents and abilities of those they lead.

2. *Evangelical subculture.* When someone visits an evangelical church, what impression do they leave with? Depending on their background, much of what is done in the worship service will be completely new to them. This is to be expected, but there are things that a pastor can do to lessen the culture shock that visitors might experience. If a church regularly has visitors who it feels are not Christians, it is good to assume that they do not know words or phrases that will be common to everyone else. A church does not want its visitors to feel any more uncomfortable than they already do (I can guarantee you that if someone is visiting your church for the first time, they will feel uncomfortable no matter what you do), so help them find something to connect to in your service. This may be as simple as acknowledging that everyone might not know what *born again, reconciliation, atonement,* or other theological words may mean. When taking an offering, one should tell those who are visiting to let the plate pass them by. If a church is having Communion and visitors are present, don't segregate them by saying if you are not a Christian, don't take the elements. Better to say, "If you are a follower of Christ, feel free to join us" (if you have open Communion). Anything a church can do to not alienate those who visit the church will increase the probability of their return. I know that churches sing songs that visitors do not know; pastors are going to preach messages from the Bible that will be unfamiliar to them. Churches cannot avoid having parts of the service that just do not relate to non-Christians. Visitors will know this and will expect a certain level of unfamiliarity, but unfamiliarity is not the same as feeling alienated.

3. *Being a leader.* Your position as pastor makes you the leader of the church, and your members will look to you to fulfill this role. Most church members want you to be a confident, strong leader but will sometimes refuse to follow your leadership depending on the issue or circumstance. And the reality is

that they do not have to follow you; there is nothing in the pastor/member relationship that requires congregations to follow where you want to take them. If your church structure is the congregational model, your members may feel a sense of independence and individuality that will work against the authority and leadership you may feel you have as the pastor. You can throw verses at your congregation that speak of how church members should follow their leaders (Hebrews 13:17 comes to mind), but if people do not want to follow you or acknowledge your and the other elder's authority (or board members), what are you going to do? You lead people who have no accountability to you; by this, I mean they can follow you or not. Unlike a work environment, where there are consequences to not doing what your superior asks, no such consequences exist in a church (except church discipline in the rare and extreme case). So how do you become an effective leader to people who can choose not to follow your leadership?

a.  **Don't flaunt your leadership or your authority.** Nobody wants to be led by someone whose style of leadership is what might be termed as "in your face." You have to earn the right to lead people, though you are given that right by the teaching of the New Testament. If your church knows that you love them and you have demonstrated this by developing personal relationships with those in your congregation and connecting with them on an emotional and sympathetic level, most of them will follow where you lead.

b.  **Don't back down once you have made a decision.** Assuming that your decision has been discussed with others, has valid reasons, and meets some need in the church, the worst thing you can do is back down if you experience some resistance or criticism of your decision.

You can lose the respect of your congregation (and your board) by changing your mind regarding a choice you have made that concerns the ministry of the church. People may complain about your decision, but they will complain more and follow you even less if they feel you do not follow through on things that you have committed to pursue.

c. **Lead with humility and grace.** These qualities are not incompatible with being a strong leader. Certainly Jesus and Paul were strong leaders, yet both of them were models of humility and grace. Humility in leadership is shown in how you communicate to your church that you are just like they are: weak, frail and dependent on God for the strength you need to lead. Grace is accepting the opinions, experiences, and ideas of others as well extending mercy, forgiveness, kindness, and acceptance. Grace also involves not judging or condemning others, especially if they do not respond to your leadership.

# Questions to Ponder

## Evangelism

1. Who are the people in your life who are not yet Christians? When can you have one of them in your home for a meal?

2. Who in your church has shown the ability and the willingness to talk to people about Christ? How might you use them to help others learn how to be successful at this endeavor?

## Evangelical Subculture

1. How comfortable do you think visitors are when they visit your church?

2.  Do you do things that make visitors stand out when they visit?

3.  Do your visitors understand everything that you say from the pulpit? Is it inevitable that they will not understand some things, or do you try and help them with the words and phrases unique to evangelicalism?

## Being a Leader

1.  Are there specific things you do as pastor to get your congregation to follow your leadership?

2.  How do you react and how do you feel when your church does not follow your lead?

3.  How do you show humility in how you lead?

4.  How does the board respond to your leadership?

# The Baptist Church

The pastor was a man named Marvin—a genial, kind, funny, and decent man who gave the church his best and was rewarded with a continued chorus of negativity by a few of the influential families in the church (by influential, I mean those who had money). His wife was the model of a pastor's wife: she played the piano, led the choir, worked with kids, and was in the language of the day "seen and not heard." The church had split under his ministry a year or so previously, but I did not know that at the time, and it would not have mattered to me anyway. I would not have known what a church split was, would not have known how this affected the church, and would not have known that the pastor of a church that splits is probably not going to be there much longer.

When churches do not grow, church members get antsy, so to speak. Because the church has in some ways absorbed the values of the culture in which it lives, American evangelical churches feel that unless they are growing, something is wrong, and they place this burden squarely on the guy in charge (many pastors are let go or leave churches because they cannot get a church to grow. I have never heard of a church dismissing the board who hired the pastor who could not get the church to grow).

I don't know how long the effort to get Marvin to leave went on, but eventually it was successful, and he was gone. I don't remember what I thought about this. I don't remember if I asked any questions or what anyone might have told me about why Marvin left, but it did not affect me that much because most of my focus at church was with the kids in the youth group. I do remember that he stood up in the pulpit one Sunday and announced to the church that the Lord had called him to another ministry and that he would be leaving (you might think that all the complainers had left. Yes and no, church splits do not follow established rules. They are messy, and sometimes people stay who have no loyalty to the pastor but cannot leave for other reasons). To me, this seemed a reasonable explanation, but I did wonder how Jesus told him to go to another church. Jesus had not yet talked to me, and I speculated that maybe He only talked to really spiritual people. Then someone told me that Jesus speaks through the Bible, but I looked around in the Bible, and I could not see any place that talked about Pastor Marvin going to another church, so I figured this was something that was beyond me. If Jesus told you to do something, you did it.

It was only much later that I came to realize that most pastors who are experiencing difficulty in their current church seem to hear from Jesus the call to move on to another church. While I do not doubt that Jesus does indeed move pastors around to different churches, He for some reason seems to mainly do it when a pastor is having difficulty, not when things are going well. Wouldn't it be something for a pastor to announce one Sunday morning, "I have been looking for some time for another church to minister in. I have finally found one, and I am out of here. I just can't seem to be able to get this church going, my ministry is not appreciated, I am tired of my wife complaining about things, so that is it. Good luck!"

Marvin went on to pastor a few more churches before he retired to Arizona, and he seemed to find a measure of happiness wherever he went. I would have occasion later in life be to involved with someone else who thought God was speaking directly to him; it would not end well.

For a church of one hundred, we had a large group of kids, and forty-five years later, I am still in contact with some of those kids, though many (including me) have moved away from southern California to other parts of the country. One of the things that was unique at that time regarding my church experience was that most of the people who attended our church were part of a family. I cannot remember any single mothers or unattached singles; all of the kids, except for me and a few who would become Christians later, were part of families that attended the church, and they represented every kind of teenager you can imagine. We had the jocks, the nerds (a nerd back then was someone who took an inordinate pleasure in school but did not care about sports; computers were decades in the future), the kids who were somewhere in between, kids who were outgoing, kids who were introverted, and one kid who never bathed and carried with him the stink of someone who does not ever take a shower. To be in a car with him was almost unbearable, especially when it was hot, and like those who develop the habit of not bathing, I doubt if he smelled his own stink. He went on to become a successful lawyer, and though I lost track of him, I assume that eventually he developed some sort of personal hygiene. Why none of us ever mentioned to him that he smelled terrible, I do not know. Kids sometimes don't have the necessary social graces needed for every situation they might encounter, though adults don't, either.

The unique thing about this group was that it seemed to work as a whole; no one was excluded, there weren't any cliques to speak of, and we had a lot of fun. Because we lived in sunny southern California, we could play outdoors nearly all year round. We had endless games of volleyball and kickball and as a group went to the beach when we could get some parent to drive us. This is not to say that our youth group were a bunch of saints. I mean, it was composed of teenage boys and girls. Some kids would actually make out during the service in the back row of the church where the adults could not see them, in plain view of the pastor who was preaching. The pastor finally called them out on this right in the middle of a sermon. You never saw heads turn around so fast. Looking back, it seems that those who were raised in Christian homes were a little less inclined toward righteousness than those of us who had come to faith on our own, as it were, without any influence from our parents. Many Christian kids have a tendency to live through the faith of their parents until they either make their own decision to follow Christ or go their own way in life, my kids included. My friend Steve, who was instrumental in my own conversion, fell away from Christ years later.

After a few months of looking for a pastor, the church called another man, a former missionary from Costa Rica. This man had started a church in Los Angeles before becoming a missionary, and he had a large family. He was very tall, somewhat outgoing, and could preach okay (like Marvin, who wore a hairpiece and had hair issues; he had a comb over that did not fool anyone). But it turned out he just could not relate to people. He could carry on conversations, visit people, was likable enough, but had no real empathy; today we would say he was an empty suit. We found out later that he took the job mainly because of the large youth group; he was concerned about his teenage son and hoped that he would find a place where he could fit in. I know that he looked at his position as pastor as a job, and you could tell that he approached his work in that way. His wife was another typical pastor's wife for that era: she played the piano, worked with kids, and did not work outside of the home. The effect that he would have on the church, including the man who would be called after him, would be long lasting and I believe eventually result in the closing of the church years down the road.

His name was Edmund, and he was unfortunately oblivious to the changes happening in the country, especially among young people, and when he finally noticed that we weren't in Kansas anymore, he had pretty much lost the youth group, though I am sure he was unaware of this at the time. I believe he had the impression or belief that if you just taught the Bible on Sunday morning all would be well with the church, and that is pretty much what he did.

It wasn't that he was a bad guy; he was just clueless. He had his concept of what a pastor was and felt that if he did what he believed was required of him that he was fulfilling the role for which he had been called. I don't believe that he ever gave any thought to growing the church or reaching out to the community; he had been successful as a missionary and church planter by doing certain things, and he would be successful as a pastor by doing what he felt the church needed here. Because he did not connect personally with people, he was not banking any goodwill that could be used by him if things at the church became difficult. Though this is true of most pastors, he did not make any real friends in the church; he had no one whom he could relate to as a man. Today it is a recognized fact that pastors need to have relationships where they can be *authentic* and *accountable* (two words that have become familiar to those in leadership but were unknown back then), but in 1970, the pastor was separated from his congregation by the idea that he was the shepherd and they were the flock, and there was a sort of firewall between them. He thought that if he kept the wheels of the church turning (service, youth group, Sunday school, Wednesday night meeting), all was well.

He began to lose us, and with us the church, about a year after he arrived. New pastors are given some time to see how they will fit into a church, how they approach ministry, and what they intend to accomplish as pastor. He came to us after a short time as our interim pastor (churches usually hire a minister to watch over the church while they are looking for a full-time pastor, an indication that most churches do not have the leadership to care for the church without someone who is "professionally" trained), and we really did not know him at all. This is the usual method for most evangelical churches in choosing a pastor; they have a number of men come and preach a sermon or two, talk to the church in some kind of special meeting, meet with the board to talk about the church's history, the former pastor (this can be an interesting conversation. Everyone has to pretend to be nice, the board has to be careful to not knock the former pastor too much or they might give the new guy pause, and the new guy has to affirm the board's decision to either let the old pastor go or agree that more could be done at the church), and then meet as a church and take some kind of vote.

My experience has been that by the time a vote is ready to be taken, the man being voted on is usually a lock. Smart leadership boards will not bring someone to a vote that they are not confident of being approved; it really makes them look bad if their candidate is not approved. Most church bylaws or constitutions have some sort of provision for bringing a man as pastor; usually it requires at least 75 percent of the congregation voting in the affirmative. Most men will not take a pastorate without at least 80-90 percent of the congregation; you want to begin your ministry on a positive note and have most of the people with you. This process can take as little as a few weeks or as long as a couple months, but the reality is that the church calls someone to be their leader who they know literally nothing about. In a work environment, the same is true, but the relationship is totally different. In a work or business setting, there are rules, procedures, set structures, a human resource department, and expectations regarding performance. Many churches hire pastors with no written expectations, no set goals, no established rules or processes that deal with communication, hours that the pastor will work, etc. The new guy is expected to grow the church and keep the membership happy. If he does this, the board and congregation usually couldn't care less when or how much the pastor works or what he does to make the church increase. The search committee has probably called some references, but these references have been provided by the pastor, so they are probably people who will not say anything bad about him, especially when they know what they say might affect his ability to get the job. Most church search committees do not talk to the previous church or the church's board to find out the real story of why the man may have left; most churches just do not want to know.

It is also the case that pastors seldom tell the real story of why they left a church. Most use phrases like, "We did not share the same vision (I could not get anyone to follow me)" or "I wanted a new challenge (I gave everything and it was time to go)" or "I felt the Lord calling me to a new ministry (I left before I they could fire me or my wife said she had had enough)." So our church ended up with Edmund, a man whom we really knew nothing about.

On a personal note, it was at this time that the military instituted the lottery system instead of using the draft to supply young men to the armed forces. It only lasted two years and then was discarded in favor of the all-volunteer army. To determine who would serve, they picked dates from a wheel, just like lottery games do, and those whose birthdays were picked first were the first to go to Vietnam. There were still some deferments available at that time, but it was thought this would make the selection of men to serve in the war more equitable. I remember sitting in front of the TV with my mom watching the numbers being picked from the container, my mouth dry and heart pounding. I had no idea what it would be like to be in Vietnam but had seen the war on the TV for the last several years and the weekly body counts. I knew that it would not be anything like a John Wayne movie, and I wasn't that far removed from *playing* with army men, let alone becoming one. Had my birthday been selected early (they were saying that anyone picked in the top fifty would be sure to go to Vietnam) and I was sent to Vietnam, if I weren't destroyed physically, I for sure would have been emotionally and mentally. I was so naïve, so relatively innocent, that serving in the military would have unalterably changed who I was as a person, as it did to many who served during those years, many against their wills. As time went on and they got farther down the list of birthdays, it became apparent that I was safe. My number ended up being 316, and I stayed safely at home.

Some of us in the youth group had heard about a church down in Costa Mesa that featured rock-and-roll music, though sung by Christian artists. You have to remember that in 1970, except for a very few Pentecostal churches, the music in your average evangelical church was organ or piano based and used hymnals featuring songs that were decades or centuries old. The music we listened to on the radio was primarily rock and roll, and when we attended church, we stepped back in time regarding music and worship. I don't think we thought this was bad; it just was the reality at the time. No one thought anything about it. Church was not supposed to be culturally relevant. That all changed after our first trip to Calvary Chapel.

At that time, Calvary was meeting in a church building seven days a week (a few months later they would set up a circus tent to accommodate the crowds). The night we came to investigate what was going on, there were about three hundred kids crammed into the auditorium. The first hour was music—rock-and-roll based songs with a Christian message sung by longhaired musicians who had been converted through the ministry of Calvary Chapel. The second hour was the pastor, Chuck Smith, sitting on a stool, teaching verse by verse through 1 Samuel. It was like at atomic bomb going off in our midst. I cannot express in words what that first service was like; it opened up a whole new world to us, one that was musically relevant, exciting, and emotionally moving. How can you not be moved when hundreds of kids are singing and dozens are going forward to be saved each night?

We would be sure to arrive early to get a seat in the front; we no doubt subconsciously thought that the closer we were, the more blessed we would be. Each night some group would play (many of them were only months old; some came together as a result of attending Calvary and finding out that other musicians were being converted), and though most of the kids in the audience had been to rock concerts, the atmosphere was nothing like what you would experience going to see the Doors or Crosby, Stills, and Nash. The music sounded the same, but the lyrics were unashamedly Christian and provoked what you might call reverent enthusiasm. Kids would sing along if they knew the words, say "amen" when a song was done, sometimes clap politely (clapping in church was absolutely not done in the early 1970s, at least not in Baptist churches—I don't remember when it became okay to clap in church), and respond to the musicians' request to be quiet during the transition to Chuck Smith teaching (imagine how hard it would be in any other circumstance to get several hundred teenagers to settle down all at once).

Chuck would then come up onto the stage and sit on a stool with some notes in front of him and teach verse by verse for about an hour. It is interesting to note that Chuck used the King James Bible when he taught to kids, kids who were experiencing constant change in their culture. (Francis Schaeffer, another man who at the same time in history was ministering to young people, also used the King James

Version.) This was before the proliferation of modern translations (another option might have been the New American Standard Bible), and the King James was undoubtedly the Bible Chuck had grown up reading and using in his ministry. Though the wording was three hundred years old and some of the words were archaic, I don't recall anyone having any problem understanding anything that he said. I would use the King James for four years before I switched to the New American Standard and the Living Bible.

One of the men who ministered at Calvary at this time was named Lonnie Frisbee (his life has been chronicled in an award-winning documentary by David Di Sabatino). Lonnie looked like Jesus, at least how Jesus was pictured in most contemporary art, with long hair, beard, a slight build, and sometimes even a robe. He was a product of the sixties, and when he was converted, he immediately began to talk to everyone he knew about Jesus, and as time went on, he began to teach at Calvary, becoming the second most recognizable leader at the church (after Chuck Smith). Lonnie would leave Calvary after a time and become involved in the Vineyard movement with John Wimber and travel across the United States and the world telling others about Jesus. It would turn out that Lonnie struggled with homosexuality during his adult life, and as Di Sabatino chronicles, would be written out of the history of both Calvary Chapel and the Vineyard movement because of his sexuality.

It seemed to me that there is no doubt that God used Lonnie during the time he was hiding his homosexuality, and I do not know quite what to think about that. I know God uses people who are sinners, but can God bless a man's ministry if he's gay? God has used others with great character flaws; history if full of Christian leaders who had tremendous ministry all the while living some sort of secret or double life. By Di Sabatino's account, Lonnie recognized this duality in his life, struggled with it, but no one was able to help him, though some may have tried. It would seem that when those in the ministry found out about his homosexuality, he was dismissed out of hand, an embarrassment to the church and the "movement."

He tragically died of AIDS in 1993, and those at his funeral thought that his fall was perhaps too prominently displayed by those who eulogized him.

Although we did not mean to, the comparisons between our church and Calvary were instantaneous, and our church did not come off well. For one thing, Chuck Smith related to kids. Though he was bald, a little overweight, and over forty, he had a twinkle in his eye and connected with every kid in the building. It is hard to explain this from a distance; it is the case of you-really-had-to-be-there. I am sure that God had something to do with this. Calvary would be the beginning of the large-scale Jesus movement in Southern California, and most that look back on that time recognize it as a form of revival. During those early years, thousands of kids converted to Christianity. Calvary Chapel would baptize those kids in the Pacific Ocean several times a year. It was quite an amazing sight to sit on the bluffs at Corona Del Mar beach and watch hundreds of kids walk into the cold water of the Pacific (though it was Southern California, during the winter and spring the ocean could get quite cool) and be baptized by men who looked like John the Baptist, who also never cut his hair.

We did not leave our church back in Orange, but some were tempted to. One of the things that Calvary offered was being baptized in the Spirit, a concept and doctrine that was foreign to most Baptist churches. It was not advertised at Calvary, but many times after the normal service they would hold an "afterglow" time, where the ministers, young men who had been converted under Chuck Smith, would lay hands on kids who desired to be baptized in the Spirit. Some of our youth group experienced this baptism and came back to our church with all the zeal of the newly converted. I watched this experience happen to a few of our kids but held back myself (God must have known that later in life I would become somewhat of a Calvinist, just a little theological humor to keep the mood light). The trouble was that when those kids came back to our church, the change in culture and relevance was unmistakable. You went from attending a church that had hundreds and then thousands in attendance, nearly all of them young kids, played music that was similar to what you listened to on the radio, had a vibrant atmosphere that was fueled by hundreds of conversions, to a church that was traditional in nature, led by a man in a suit who just could not connect with anyone, and sang hymns that were relevant musically (and sometimes lyrically) to generations long since gone.

By this time everyone knew what was going on at Calvary, and though it was hard for the adults to be negative about the youth group going down to Calvary (how do you tell your kid they cannot go to church, especially when it did not conflict with your own church services?), some of the adults did have reservations. After all, they were playing rock music, and many of the musicians had long hair and looked uncomfortably like *hippies* (a word that has more or less died in our culture). Unless you lived during that time, it is difficult to appreciate what parents went through in the late sixties and early seventies. Most schools had dress codes, which included hair length for guys, and some parents saw rock music (even in a Christian context) as part of the devil's strategy to corrupt America's youth. So we had this tension that was beginning to develop in the youth group, and while many of the adults had the good sense to realize that the best thing to do was to support the kids and give them some direction and advice when it was appropriate, the pastor was caught completely off guard and reacted in the worst manner possible, by trying to control and even stifle the kids' newfound zeal.

It is hard to explain how fast the culture was changing during those years; values, morals, and beliefs were being questioned on a daily basis by the younger generation, and parents were constantly being probed by their kids about what they believed. Many parents could not coherently explain to their kids either why what they believed was true or why what their kids believed was wrong. People today are much more accustomed to rapid change due to the invasiveness of technology, which can begin a trend overnight.

One of the worst things that can happen in a church is doctrinal division. Most churches have a specific theological tradition that has been developed over many years, is usually the result of some event in the church's or denomination's past, and are wary of anyone who would hold to a different view on a specific doctrine or teaching (most denominations feel that their doctrinal distinctions are based on what the Bible teaches, but honestly, somebody has to be wrong). The main evangelical denominations have all been formed around their specific views on some of these debated issues; reformed churches generally follow a Calvinistic theology; others follow a more Arminian theology (Methodist, Wesleyan, Nazarene, Foursquare); Lutherans have their own doctrinal leanings.

Which brings us to the Pentecostal/Charismatic movement, which believes in outward manifestations (speaking in tongues, baptism of the Spirit) that at the time found no place in your typical Baptist church (there are now charismatic Baptist churches, charismatic Presbyterian churches, even charismatic Catholic churches). So what does a Baptist pastor do when some of the kids in his youth group become advocates for a rock-and-roll type of worship and have been baptized in the Spirit and are occasionally speaking in tongues? He freaks out, that's what he does! I can imagine Edmund running to the board and telling them, "You never said anything about kids being baptized in the Spirit! Or speaking in tongues! How could you parents let this happen? That's not in my job description (if he had a job description)!" My guess is that he thought he was coming to a relatively quiet backwater of a church where he could play it safe for a few years, but God is not concerned about our personal "safety."

Well, the fact was the parents were just as surprised by this as he was, though some of them had the sense to sit back and watch what was happening and try to be as encouraging as possible, directing the zeal instead of trying to stifle it, which is what Edmund tried to do. Actually, I think this whole episode had to do with emotion and the place of it in the life of young believers. Many Baptists are wary of emotion, and though they will yell their lungs out at a sporting event (think of Southern Baptists going to high school football games on Friday nights in Texas), to get them to clap their hands or raise them in a service, that was just not done. Most of the kids who got caught up in the Calvary experience were not the kids who had family members in the church, but the new kids (like me) who had come into the youth group in the last year or so and were more open to learning new things about their faith. Certainly there was much passion on the part of these kids, but passion is not a bad thing, as most NFL fans will tell you. I think that Edmund had an idea of how church should be experienced, and though that included some emotion at the appropriate times (some churches today try to manage and manipulate their congregation's emotions through the use of music, video, and lighting, though they would not say it that way), it did not include any outward manifestations of the Holy Spirit that were outside of his theological understanding. He decided to meet with the youth and try to show how speaking in tongues and being baptized in the Spirit were not Baptist doctrines, but he did not get very far.

It is very rare to have a church that has both charismatic and non-charismatic adherents; it does not seem that these two groups of people can coexist together in harmony. These were not doctrines that were in any way considered heresy, but he drew a line in the sand when he said that the kids were wrong in what they believed and that as their pastor they should be willing to accept his view on these teachings (I don't think he said it exactly like that, but that is what he meant and how it came across). The end result was that some of the kids left the church and went to Calvary Chapel. This process lasted a couple months and was viewed with sadness by many of the adults, who had appreciated the new life that was brought into the church by these kids who had been saved in the last year or so. I never thought of leaving the church. I was too close to Steve's family, had been attending for almost three years, and though I continued to go to Calvary Chapel on a regular basis, I never became a charismatic.

Edmund's honeymoon period had long since been over, and there were rumblings among the adults about how he was doing as pastor. I have mentioned his lack of relating to people on any type of emotional level, his lack of vision for the church, and his continuance of the status quo, but there occurred one event that brought together those who had a growing concern with his ministry. Most evangelical churches have in the summer some type of Vacation Bible School in which they run a program that is designed especially for kids who do not attend church. The thought is to get the kids to enjoy coming to church, have fun with other kids, and then in a closing program have the parents come and see how the kids enjoyed the program, how nothing bad happens when you go inside a church, and then invite them to attend the church so their kids can keep having fun (if you believed what today's media says about evangelicals, the odds are that you would never darken the doors of an evangelical church).

It has now been recognized that these types of programs do not bring many new families into the church, but tradition is a powerful force, and most churches still have some type of Vacation Bible School. Many parents who do not attend church look forward to the summer when churches hold their Vacation Bible Schools; they serve as free daycare for a week, and who really minds the kids learning a little about the Bible as long as we (the parents) don't have to go to church? We had our annual Vacation Bible School, and on Friday night we had the wrap-up meeting with the parents where the kids performed songs, did some skits, and generally showed to their parents what a good time they had. Edmund then got up and thanked the parents for allowing their kids to come, said some things about the church, and closed in prayer.

So you are thinking, *Okay, what's the big deal?* Unless you come from a Baptist church or a church with similar tradition, you might have noticed that Edmund did not give a gospel invitation to those who were present. Everyone in the church knew that there were many parents present who were not Christians; the whole purpose of the Vacation Bible School was to get parents in the church to hear about Jesus. Here they were, but they did not hear anything about Jesus.

For some in the church, this was literally unforgivable. Our church gave an invitation at every service, even when there were no visitors and no possibility of anyone going forward for salvation (think of the unspoken impact of having an invitation week after week where no one ever goes forward. Tradition can be a terrible thing; you just keep doing something because you have always done it, no matter that it brings no results). I don't know what Edmund was thinking as he stood in the pulpit and knew that there were no visitors who might need to be saved and come forward when he gave an invitation. Sometimes he would ask people to just raise their hands to indicate some kind of response to his invitation; the kids would usually open their eyes to see who had raised their hands and was in some sort of spiritual need.

Another tradition the church had: the pastor sat on a small pew on the stage next to the pulpit and not with the congregation. This had the subtle effect of saying he was different from the congregation and needed a special place to sit. So to not have an invitation when there were non-Christians sitting right there in the pews, this could not be allowed to pass without some kind of discussion. I have no idea who called the meeting, but it happened on Wednesday night when the church met for Bible study and youth group. Edmund realized that there was some intense feeling about his lack of giving an invitation and may have sensed that he was in a bit of trouble, so as a church, we met and discussed what had happened.

What it boiled down to was this: many people thought that he had blown it by not offering an invitation; Edmund said he had not felt led to do that (how do you argue a point when someone says that God lead them to do or not do something?) and let people have their say. There was some conversation about the overall tenor of his ministry, which I do not think took him completely by surprise, and the upshot of all this was that he ended up taking a few days off to go out to the desert to fast and pray and seek God's guidance for his ministry. Not the literal desert but a motel in the desert near Palm Springs, though he did drive out to places in the desert where he could be alone. No doubt he took his inspiration from John the Baptist or Moses.

I will say that he came back from this experience with a passion that he had not exhibited before; this was mainly seen in his preaching. His new directness and changed demeanor were not lost on the congregation, and we appreciated the change in his heart, but the die had been cast, and he would be gone in a few months. I never talked with him about how he arrived at the decision to leave the church, though I would have plenty of opportunity to do so in the years to come, as our lives would intersect at many different points in the future. He left the church to take a position at a Bible college in another state and was only at the church for two years. During this time, there was no growth; indeed, along with those kids that fled for Calvary Chapel, a few families just did not respond to Edmund and joined other churches in the area. So the church again geared up to search for a new pastor. This time I would be included on the pastoral search committee as a representative from the youth.

Looking for a pastor is an exercise fraught with hidden dangers that involve both the candidate and the church. Most churches begin by assembling a number of resumes of men looking for new ministry opportunities, getting these resumes either from the denomination or various seminaries or Bible colleges. Most of the time, from what I can tell, the two parties are unknown to each other before the process begins. So as a search committee, we looked through a number of resumes and picked three or four that seemed to have promise. The first man we had come to the church was from our denomination and was a chaplain in the military. He preached one Sunday morning as a candidate, by which you would assume that he would preach his best sermon. I was sitting in the choir loft listening (my children will be wondering why anyone would let me be in a choir, but you have to remember it was a small church) to him preach. All I remember was that he could speak okay, but he never once mentioned the word *Jesus* in his sermon. There may have been a reason for this, but for a new Christian like me, it was odd that you could speak for forty-five minutes and not mention Christ. He did not connect with anyone, and so we brought in another man. I don't think it helped that the first candidate was about the same age as Edmund; it may have been that subconsciously we were leaning for a younger man, though this was never stated as a prerequisite for becoming our pastor (today you would be breaking the law if you listed as one of your criteria for a minister that he be of a certain age).

The next man was right out of seminary and was currently managing a McDonald's restaurant in the Bay area (which was a plus in my book; the Big Mac had just been introduced, and I loved them). He came down for the weekend, and as we met with him Saturday evening, we found he was everything that Edmund was not. He was articulate, had many different ideas for the church, projected an infectious enthusiasm, seemed to be able to relate to us on a more personal level, and asked us many questions about the church and its current circumstances and past history. One of the things that struck all of us was that he said a church like ours should double in size in a year or so, like that was not a big deal. We did not ask him how he would accomplish that, a big mistake on our part. Had he really known how to accomplish that he could have either written a book or held conferences on church growth and made a bundle and become famous.

We called him a week later after discussing him with the assembled church and taking a vote, which was unanimous. Because this was his first church, there were no ministerial references we could check to see how he was functioned as a pastor, but we did call his personal references, who all said what a wonderful guy he was. Again, who puts down as references someone who will say anything negative about you? It's similar to being a lawyer; lawyers never ask a question in court unless they know how the witness is going to answer, so any candidate for a church will only list those as references that he knows will speak well of him.

There was a telling incident during his candidacy that I would remember years later. When we were talking with him and his wife on Saturday night, after an hour or so, she just casually mentioned that the watch he was wearing did not even work. He immediately turned to her and tried to quiet her, in a playful manner, but you could see that he was upset; he perceived that she had made him look bad. I remember thinking, *Why would you wear a watch that did not work?* It wasn't the last question that I would ask about him.

His name was Matthew, and he would end up being at the church just a little longer than Edmund, and when he left the church, he was on his way to leaving the ministry. What does seminary do to young men (and now women)? They come out of school with little or no experience in being the pastor of a church and think that they are qualified to lead a group of disparate individuals to maturity as believers and reach out to the lost as well, bringing them into the church and growing them in the faith because they have training and a degree.

I have lived in the world of Bible college and seminary graduates for over forty years now and have watched these graduates step into churches and have varying degrees of success and failure. For one thing, seminary does not actually prepare you to do anything substantial except preach the Bible; its primary purpose is to teach its students the Bible, its languages, its doctrines, its history, its culture, etc. What it does not do is teach you how to work with people, teach a small group, train leaders, lead a meeting, disciple a new believer, be a leader of people, and provide vision—really anything practical. It should be obvious to anyone paying attention that seminaries and Bible colleges cannot do this because they are divorced from the real world of churches. You can teach a class on how to disciple a new believer or how to lead a church through change, but because the class is held in a world of students and teachers and not lay people who have jobs, have never attended a seminary, and have never read a book by Dallas Willard, it can in no way prepare those students for the real world of churches. Seminaries have made steps in this direction by trying to provide internships to its students and requiring them to have some practical experience in a church to graduate, but these are recent changes that not all seminaries have instituted.

The role of the seminary still seems to be how to get people to understand what the Bible teaches, a worthy goal, but only part of what a pastor actually does. Because most of the people the pastor will minister to will not have been to seminary or Bible college, it is a very real temptation to think that because you know more than the man in the pew, you are the smartest guy in the room, though no one would ever be so crass as to say this out loud. This was probably truer in the 1970s than now, and Matthew would reflect that superiority in a number of ways, but can you really blame him? He was just the product of a system that churches and denominations supported as the way to train pastors and equip them for ministry. The thought that God might be able to equip someone to lead a church outside of formal training was a thought that was never seriously entertained then, though there has been some movement in that direction in recent years. The most telling statistic about the effectiveness of seminaries and Bible colleges in training people for church ministry is that a majority of pastors quit the ministry within five years of graduation.

Matthew jumped in with both feet, and you could feel the energy that he brought to the church. New people began to show up, there were more events at the church, and he began to change the way the service was done. He played the guitar and sang, so he incorporated these into the Sunday evening service and began to have spontaneous times when people could share prayer requests and personal insights right in the service. He had read Ray Stedman's book *Body Life* and brought some of these principles into our church. It seemed like he did everything—teaching the youth on Sunday morning, doing the teaching Wednesday night, preaching Sunday evening, singing at least once a month. He was a bundle of energy.

Pastors have always had difficulty making friends with those they minister to; there is some kind of unspoken rule that the pastor cannot be real or genuine with this congregation lest they come to see him as just a person and not some great spiritual leader. I understand the need to be busy doing things—as a seminary student you just spent three or four years studying and thinking—but building relationships with people is like having money in the bank. When times get tough, those relationships can help get you through misunderstandings or difficulties with people. I think that a lot of his energy masked a lack of spiritual reality in his own life, which he made up for in busyness.

There was one thing that you were sure of: he was the boss. Though only twenty-six years old and right out of school, he made it clear that he was in charge, though he was not overbearing about it. My guess is that he felt that if he took or asked for advice from the deacon board (or anyone else) it would make him seem weak or not sure of himself. So he never projected any weakness or doubt or indecision. Who can live like this? To always be in charge, to always be right, to always be the "man": no one, especially a kid right out of school with no practical experience in the job he was doing, is that strong emotionally. Pastors are now more frequently allowed to be human (what a strange thing to say), and many, but not all, churches today recognize that pastors can be honest about their limitations and the need for peer friendship and help them live according to expectations that are realistic and reachable.

Because Matthew was bringing new ideas and practices into the church, he frequently met with the board to explain what he was doing. Our board consisted of three men, all successful in the business world, who were at least fifteen years older than Matthew. They were decent men but needed to be persuaded about things; they did not merely rubber stamp everything Matthew wanted to do. Here again, Matthew could have won these men over had he showed a little grace and humility toward them, bringing them along instead of pushing them along. It was always "We need to do this now" with him. He should have known that, with a traditional church, you have to finesses some things in order to get what you think the church might need; but then, they didn't teach him that in seminary, either.

At the church, things had settled into a routine, both for the church and for Matthew. Outwardly, things appeared to be going well; there were new people attending, the offerings were up, but he was not able to get along with his board. They did not have any real conflicts or shouting matches; he just marginalized them and viewed the men, not as part of a team, but rather as a group who needed to be taught and led, just like the rest of the church. The board was still composed of three men who were pretty mature and not inclined to conflict, but they did not like Matthew's attitude very much, and at least one of the men tried to tell him how he was coming across.

During one meeting, a board member mentioned to Matthew that the church did not believe in papal infallibility. The remark was intended to convey to Matthew that he might not always be right on everything, but the words went right over his head, and he responded with only a bemused smile. The board member did not pursue the matter. If the board had just been honest with Matthew about how he was coming across to them and opened a dialogue with him that could have helped him grow, one wonders how things might have turned out differently for him. We are seldom really honest in a gracious manner with those who are pastors and leaders; we are afraid of offending them, questioning their leadership, or having any type of conflict. As a result, when there is conflict, it usually comes in the form of a crisis of some sort, with the attending fallout that unresolved and spontaneous conflict often brings.

When I came back in the summer from attending Bible college in another state, Matthew had done something that brought a lot of these issues to a head. He had approached someone in the church about a behavior that he thought needed to be addressed (I cannot remember what it was) and had not been perhaps as humble and tactful as he could have been, and feelings were hurt. In and of itself, this is not out of the ordinary; people get their feelings hurt all the time in any number of relationships, churches included. But Matthew was adamant that he had done nothing wrong; he was merely following biblical guidelines in trying to help a member of his flock with a behavior that he considered wrong (he may have been right in how he interpreted the Bible and in the need to help someone correct a sinful behavior, but like many things in life, it is not what you do but how you do it that makes your actions successful or not). Being a small church, this conflict got around, and the board was called in to see if things could be straightened out, and the issue might have been resolved if only Matthew had just listened to the counsel of someone other than himself.

So it was during our regular Wednesday night church gathering that he had everyone come into the auditorium from their classes and youth group so that he could address us about this issue. I had only been back a few weeks from school and really did not know at that point what was going on. I was sitting in the back with my girlfriend (Steve's stepsister, who I would marry the next summer) while Matthew talked about the role of a pastor and how it was like that of a shepherd. He held in his hand a staff of some kind as a prop and was saying how shepherds sometimes have to be gentle with the sheep, and sometimes harsh, for their own good. As he spoke the word *harsh*, he brought the staff down in a swift motion on one of the pews, and I am not exaggerating when I tell you that everyone nearly jumped out of their seats. He then began ranting about following the shepherd, but no one was really listening. The act of bringing that staff down suddenly, with the loud noise that it created in a room that was already quiet and tense, was just electric. His wife started to cry. The tension in the room exploded like a bomb. Some other women began to cry, some went to try and comfort Matthew's wife, some were shaking their heads, not believing what they had heard and witnessed, and Matthew just kept talking even though he had lost the moment and no one was really listening. Being in the back, I could see everything that was happening and was so appalled that I just left with my girlfriend to go back to her house. I have always been averse to conflict, and it seemed that there was no way that the evening was going to end well, so I just left.

Later, when my girlfriend's parents returned home from church, we talked about what had happened. They knew that they needed to provide some kind of context for us to be able to process this incident; I mean, it isn't every day that the pastor goes kind of ballistic, accusing people of not following him and trying to undermine his ministry. Their reaction was a display of maturity and grace that is seldom seen in churches. They knew that he was a young man, that he was probably somewhat insecure about himself, and their response to his display of authority and arrogance was, and I will never forget these words, *We'll just love him to death.* He (my future father-in-law) was head of the deacon board and probably could have gotten Matthew fired if he wanted after that night, but he didn't. They wanted to try and save him and knew that the best and perhaps only way to do that was to forgive him, love him, and see if he could be smoothed out around the edges. In most churches, that would have been the end of Matthew, but not here.

Matthew had no intention of leaving. In his mind he had done nothing wrong; he was merely exercising his function as pastor, and the thought that the board might dismiss him probably never entered his mind. The reaction from most people was that he was totally inappropriate in how he manipulated that meeting, with the staff and all, and several people told him so. But in his mind, this would just confirm that there was more work for him to do; until people understood that everything he was doing was for their good, he had a long way to go. Such is the twisted logic of those who feel that they cannot do any wrong. It is hard to believe, but this eventually blew over, though his ministry would not be the same. He had emotionally lost quite a few people, and though no one left the church (those who attended Wednesday night were the core group of the church, and they tended to value the relationships they had developed with others over the years) things were not the same. Many people never knew what happened that Wednesday night, and so their perception of Matthew was still the same.

I was back at school in the fall, and things at the church returned to a kind of normal. The church continued on the same path, growing slowly, but Matthew was beginning to show the strain of living under his own expectations. If you remember, he confidently told the search committee that the church should double in a year or so, and this was obviously not going to happen. A lot of the happiness we have as people is found in how our reality matches our expectations in life, and his reality was much less than his expectation in terms of what he thought would happen at the church. And if your expectations are not met, then you look for reasons why they have not been met, and the blame game begins. In this case, the simple proposition was that either Matthew was to blame or the church was to blame. There is a third alternative: that no one was to blame and that there were other circumstances in the life and history of the church that were factors in how it was growing and developing. But in Matthew's mind, I am sure that the thought that he could not work with these people was beginning to grow, that they were not responding to his leadership or doing what he asked, and so the trend would continue where another pastor would be gone before he had spent five years at the church (the average stay for a pastor in that denomination is less than five years).

I came back to the church the following summer after another year at school and would be married in July. Things at church had settled into a routine; there had not been any significant events during the year at church. It may be that Matthew had just settled into a pattern that he found comfortable. The church reached a high point in terms of numbers that year, so you'd think that Matthew would have found a measure of satisfaction in that, but I don't think that he did. He had no real friends (a common trait among many pastors) and took too much of his identity from his work. I don't know if he felt like a failure or not, but he had lost some of the initial enthusiasm he had brought to the work. Because he was going to marry my wife and me, we had to go to him for counseling. We only went for one session (his idea), and he talked to us about three things: money, in-laws, and sex. He said that these were the areas in which couples usually had problems (I could not imagine having any problems regarding sex with my beautiful fiancée, but did not say so), so he kind of went over each area in some detail. Being young and naïve, I did not think that we would have any problems in our marriage (which would pretty much turn out to be true; I give my wife all the credit for this), but we listened politely.

It turned out that he gave the same speech to another couple who was going to get married in the church around the same time we were. The groom to be was a friend of mine, and after he and his fiancée met with Matthew, we compared notes and found out that what he said to each of us was almost word for word the same. He did not ask us any questions, he did not try to engage us (no pun intended) in any type of give-and-take conversation, and he basically just preached us a sermon on sex, in-laws, and money as it related to the newly married. He was not a good listener, but then few people are. When he married us in July, it would officially mark the end of my involvement in that church. The one thing that I remember about what he said in his message during the wedding was that it might be possible for us to drift apart and have the marriage end in divorce. I thought that this was really inappropriate but was so excited to be married that I let it pass.

Living in the early 1970s, many Bible teachers, Chuck Smith among them, were confident that Christ was going to return at literally any moment. I must confess to hoping that His return would hold off until at least after our honeymoon.

Our marriage would not end in divorce, but Matthew's did. Matthew left the ministry after another pastorate and went into business. I lost track of him until I did an Internet search and found that he was divorced and living in the Midwest.

## Principles for the Pastor

1. *Leaving a church.* Most pastors do not leave a church when things are going well. Those with some experience will know when things at a church are going downhill and begin to plan an exit strategy, trying to stay ahead of the curve, as it were. Most of the time they do not tell anyone about their plans to leave, which is not surprising since some churches would more than likely dismiss a man who had decided to leave.

If things have gotten so bad that a pastor must leave, and there is no possibility of working out whatever difficulties may exist in his ministry, then he may not have any other choice than to look for a church without informing his board. This is not the best option, but it is an option. If he feels that he can trust his board, he can let them know he would like to pursue other options in ministry and give them his reasons for doing so. This may open up a dialogue about his current position and create a situation where he might be able to stay and find some renewal and support. I realize this is his income we are talking about, but income should never be the main reason anyone makes decisions regarding ministry. Every time a pastor leaves a church when things have not gone well, he approaches the next church with a little less trust, a little less energy, and a little less faith in those he will work with. The best way to avoid leaving a church under a cloud is to begin and end well. More on this later.

2. *Setting the tone for the church.* Pastors do this by how they preach, what they preach on, and how they live their lives. Churches should be places where people find acceptance, comfort, and, most importantly, grace. By this I mean that churches should be places that make those who attend feel they are unconditionally loved by God. You might ask, how can pastors make people feel like they are not loved and accepted by God? The answer is that many churches, led by the pastor, often equate the Christian life with a set of rules that believers need to follow in order to be "spiritual." In some cases, these rules are even spelled out in the church documents. In the case of the church I attended after becoming a Christian, members were not permitted to dance, drink, or smoke; it was written right in the church bylaws. These practices were at that time indications of being "unspiritual." Notice these are all outward practices, things that can be easily seen and hence judged.

Many pastors preach the same basic message over and over again: God is good, you are bad, try harder. This causes members to feel that the more obedient they are, the more God loves them. Pastors sometimes feel that if they preach that God loves His children unconditionally, it will lead his congregation to live any way they want. In fact, it usually does the exact opposite, freeing the church to live without the feeling that God is watching everything they do, ready to pounce if they misbehave. If pastors preach the grace of God and His love for His children, people will respond with a renewed sense of wonder at what God has done for them in Christ.

3.  *The absence of friends.* This has had the result of making many pastors feel isolated, without any friends or peers whom they can talk and relate to. Some pastors do this by choice, others by default. One of my best friends realized that as a pastor he needed a place to relate to other men and started an accountability group with several other men in his church that has now lasted over five years. Many pastors just will not do this; they do not want others to know they have the same weaknesses, temptations, or difficulties as they do, feeling such an admission will weaken their ministry. If you are a pastor and feel this way, shame on you. You are putting yourself above others in your church, avoiding the opportunity to let others minister to you and setting yourself up for failure. If you absolutely feel you cannot find a group in your church to join in terms of relating to others, then find a group of ministers that you can join to find the care and relationship you need, and be sure to let your board know you are in a group that is helping you grow as a disciple.

4.  *How to deal with doctrinal division.* It seems every church will deal with leaders or members (or the pastor) who will have divergent doctrinal views. Although most people attend

churches that they agree with doctrinally, occasionally there will be issue that will arise that can catch the pastor and the leadership off guard. The first thing to determine is if the doctrinal issue is foundational or just a difference of opinion on a matter that has been recognized by the church as having various legitimate interpretations. Foundational issues that are currently being debated in the evangelical church are open theism, denial of hell, universalism, inerrancy, and the debate concerning homosexuality. Doctrinal issues that are perhaps more matters of interpretation are prophecy, lordship salvation, issues of church government and management, and the ordination of women to the ministry (though some view this as a foundational issue). Does the church have a position on whatever the issue is? Does the denomination? If so, this is the place to start in beginning a dialogue.

Notice that I used the word *dialogue*. When people bring different interpretations of the Bible into the church, it is best to address them directly and quickly. Pastors must lead on this and graciously show what the church believes, and with the board find a way to either accept or reject the new teaching. This is in no way rejecting people, but leaders do have a responsibility to guard the doctrine of the church. *Don't do things (like sit up on the platform above the people) that separate you from the congregation.* If a pastor wants to wear a robe when they preach, fine, but realize that if no one else is wearing a robe, what does this say to the members? A pastor's gifts are to be used to benefit and mature the congregation; the position already has set him apart from everyone else; he must find ways to communicate he is are just like everyone else, a sinner saved by grace, loved and accepted by God.

5. *Pastors need times of spiritual refreshment.* It will help restore focus and bring added life and spiritual energy. I am not talking about a vacation, which is also necessary. I am thinking about times spent in prayer, fasting, and extended reading and

meditating on the Bible. This is necessary because the job has responsibilities and temptations that other occupations just do not share. The board should understand this and allow time off for this pursuit. When going to a new church, ask if this can be a part of the employment contract.

6. The Pastor and the Board, Part One: *How do you get along with your board?* The answer to this question will determine to a large measure how successful your ministry will be. Here are some suggestions on how to manage this relationship.

   a. **Be honest with the board.** Pastors should communicate with their boards how they are doing spiritually and how the feel about the ministry.

   b. In the board meetings, **have some personal time to share prayer requests** that are centered on the personal details of each member's life: work, families, temptations, successes, and failures. Do not limit board meetings to just issues of the church.

   c. **Define the role of the board** so that everyone agrees on how it will function. It may take a retreat or an extended time together to do this, but it will pay benefits in the long term.

   d. **Consider meeting less.** Boards that meet more than twice a month (unless there are special circumstances such as looking for a new pastor) probably dwell too much on the details of the church and not on vision, policy, or goals. The details of the church should be left to the pastor and/or staff, with the board overseeing the pastor. This may be a new thought for some pastors. For more information on a model for church boards that is becoming common in evangelical churches, Google "Carver Governance Model."

e.  Although it will be difficult, **try not to cater to those on the board who may be rich.** I have seen this happen in churches: some board members who happen to be well off seem to expect to be treated differently by the pastor and may want more influence in the affairs of the church. Ask God for wisdom in how to deal with each of your board members; He will help those who ask to act with integrity and wisdom.

# Questions to Ponder

## Leaving the Church

1.  What reasons or circumstances would cause you to leave your church?

2.  Do you see anything like this in your current situation?

3.  How attached are you to the income your church provides? How would the potential loss of income influence what you might do to stay at your church?

4.  If money were not an issue, would your family prefer you find another job?

5.  If you asked your board this question, "How much longer do you think the pastor will be at the church," how would they answer?

## Setting the Tone for Your Church

1.  How do you promote the following qualities in your church?

    a.  Acceptance

    b.  Love

    c.  Grace

   d.   Holiness

   e.   Compassion

2.   What might some words that characterizes the tone of your church? Chose from the following list:

   a.   Gracious

   b.   Loving

   c.   Accepting

   d.   Tolerant

   e.   Compassionate

   f.   Legalistic

   g.   Separate

   h.   Fearful

   i.   Judgmental

   j.   Isolated

3.   If your board members set the tone for the church, what might that look like?

4.   How would people say your sermons reflect the tone of your church?

*Friends*

1.   Name your close friends in the church.

2.   Who would you turn to if your teenage daughter ran away?

3.   Do you belong to a small group of other men where you are not the leader?

4. Are any of your board members your friends?

5. Do you feel it is possible to make friends at your church?

6. Do you have other pastors who are your close friends?

7. What do you think might be missing in your life if you do not have any close friends?

## Doctrinal Division

1. How have you dealt or not dealt with doctrinal division in the past?

2. What doctrines or teachings can you allow other people in your church to hold, and what doctrines do you consider foundational? For example:

   a. Ordination of women to the ministry

   b. Baptism in the Spirit

   c. Calvinism

   d. Denial of hell

   e. Theistic evolution

   f. Old/young earth

   g. Open theism

   h. Mode of baptism

   i. Church government

   j. Inerrancy

   k. Universalism

3. How monolithic in their beliefs is your board? What are their views of the above issues? Is your church's doctrinal statement too narrow or too broad? Do you exclude people from membership if they have different interpretations of doctrines in your doctrinal statement?

## Times of Spiritual Refreshment

1. When was the last time you spent a few days alone to read, pray, fast, and meditate on the Bible?

2. Do you think you need times like this at regular intervals?

3. When could you do this in the coming year?

4. Would your board and family support you in this type of practice?

5. On a scale of 1 to 10, rate the reality of your spiritual experience today.

6. Do you honestly think time away spent in this type of endeavor would benefit you?

## The Board: Part One

1. On a scale of 1 to 10, how well are you getting along with your board?

2. If you could replace certain board members, would you? Which ones? Why?

3. Do you treat board members differently than you treat the rest of your church? What does this look like practically ? If so, why?

4. What do your board members do that diminishes your role as pastor? Have you expressed this to them?

5.  How do you view your board, as more of a team or a necessary evil?

6.  How does your relationship with the board affect your overall ministry?

# The Other Baptist Church

During my first two years at the Bible college, when I was not married, I attended a few different churches. You had to be involved in some form of Christian service while you were in school, so most kids found a church where they could serve. For my first year I volunteered to serve not in a church but in a ministry that tried to reach out to kids in the inner city. This ministry would rent local indoor basketball courts from the school district and invite kids to come and play together on the condition that they listen to a short message at halftime. Some were more than kids. They were in their late teens or early twenties; we were afraid to exclude them because they brought younger kids who looked up to them. They were pretty well armed, as well. They carried switchblade knives, and they talked a lot about guns, and though we did not ever see any guns, they did bring large gym bags to each game. They were almost all involved in gangs and drugs and made it clear they had no interest in anything that we said; they were just there to play basketball. Sometimes they would not even let us play in the games, so we just watched.

One time when I did get into a game, I spent the evening guarding this one young Hispanic kid who was pretty good, routinely beating me to the basket and telling me how lousy I was. As the evening wore on, I was having a really good time despite the fact that they were rather disruptive and rude during halftime. When I got back to the dorm later that evening, I took off my T-shirt, and as it went over my head, I noticed that it smelled funny and I burst out laughing hysterically for no reason. It turns out that the kid had been smoking marijuana right before the game, and maybe during halftime, and by being close to him for about two hours, I had somehow inhaled some secondhand pot breath and gotten a little high. Because I had never smoked marijuana before (or any other drug or alcohol for that matter), it probably had more of an effect on me that it might have had on someone else. My roommates and I thought this was extremely funny (at that point I would have thought anything extremely funny), and as I remember back, it took me awhile to get to sleep that night.

The next year I went to a small Baptist church similar to the one I attended in California and taught the high school group on Sunday mornings. It turned out that I was a good communicator, and the kids seemed to enjoy our time together. This was a good experience for me. I got my feet wet doing a type of ministry that I was suited for, and because the church was about the same as where I had come from, it was a pretty easy transition.

My involvement in the church was limited during that last year at school to Sunday mornings; we would teach the high school class and attend the morning worship service but were not able to come to Wednesday night youth group, which another couple was responsible for. Going to Bible college was kind of like going to church every day, so we did not think it strange to be only casually involved during that time; plus we had many friends through the school that we socialized with, relationships that for us fulfilled the need that church had provided back in California. It was during that final year at school that my wife became pregnant. Just about the time I graduated, she developed complications and had to be on bed rest for the final three months of her pregnancy. I had gotten a job at a local retail outlet right after graduating and was just able to support us, though it was financially tight. The church was a real help during this time; the ladies brought meals and visited on a regular basis. These acts of kindness helped to confirm for us that this was where we should be going to church; having graduated from school, the requirement for Christian service was gone, and we could have attended another church with many of our school friends, but we chose to remain there instead. I had begun discipling two of the high school kids and did not want to lose those relationships, as well as my regular teaching on Sunday morning.

The church did not take long to find another pastor. Because the church had a good relationship with the seminary in the city, they were able to go right to the president of that school and ask him to recommend someone for the position. He was more than obliging. He sent a young man to us who had been his personal assistant and had just graduated. I don't think the church looked at anyone else; there was no one else who came to preach or candidate. I mean, if you are going to ask the president of the seminary in your own denomination for a personal favor, I suppose you better take the person that he recommends. Having just graduated from Bible college myself, I think that in some respect I had an unconscious affinity for someone who had just spent years studying the Bible. Had I forgotten about Matthew? Apparently.

It is hard to explain to people what going to Bible college or seminary is like. You basically remove yourself from the real world for a number of years and become immersed in a place that in some respects has no basis in reality. This sounds harsh, but it is true nonetheless. Because the seminary or Bible college has no connection to churches, it stands completely separate as an institution. The men and women it trains to fill the ministry of these churches live and breathe in a world that they will not inhabit when they graduate. To put it another way, seminaries and Bible colleges do not need churches in order to function (they do need the money that churches and denominations provide, but to actually train students they have everything that need). Because churches do not train those who end up leading them (pastors, associate pastors, etc.), there is a huge disconnect between the church and the institutions that provide the men and women who work in those churches. Many times (indeed, I would say most of the time), those who end up becoming the pastor of a church come in knowing nothing about those they are going to lead, little about the history of the church, little or nothing about the dynamics of how the church works, who are the biggest givers, who are the main families, who are interrelated, and who has caused problems in the past, and the church knows little or nothing about the person who becomes their pastor.

What institutions also accomplish is to help perpetuate the idea that only those who have attended these institutions are qualified to lead or pastor churches, which can then lead to the idea that these graduates are more spiritual, more mature, and more gifted than the people that they lead. (When pastors go to conferences with other pastors, the first question they usually ask is, "Where did you go to school?" followed by "How big is your church?") What else are they supposed to think? They have spent years devoted solely to understanding the Bible, giving of their time, energy, and fortunes to become equipped to lead and shepherd others in their own spiritual journey. The problem is that without a measure of grace, humility, maturity, vision, confidence, and emotional depth, all of that knowledge is worthless in the real world. There is also the matter of being "called" to the ministry. Because most pastors feel a special calling from God to do ministry, this also separates them from the congregation. I mean, who has ever been "called" to sell insurance in the same way a pastor feels he is called to do God's work. Churches can be messy, difficult, and are full of people with hidden agendas, resistant to change and with traditions and dynamics that take time to discover. You cannot learn these things in a class in seminary, especially when the information you are getting about how to run a church is held in an institution that in itself is set apart from the church.

Jeffrey was not Matthew, but he was close. Just like Matthew, he had just graduated from seminary, he was young and had a wife who did not work outside the home, and he was full of energy. One difference was that Jeffrey had a little more depth and maturity than Matthew and was perhaps less insecure. He was genuinely interested in people, did not have quite the manic energy that Matthew exhibited, and had a sense of humor. This is not to say that he did not have the same attitude that Matthew had about those who have graduated from seminary. He had spent four years going to seminary, had been the personal assistant to the president of the seminary, and now was chosen to lead a church that was pretty traditional and conservative. He had his work cut out for him.

One of the most difficult things a pastor can do is to change the culture and philosophy of ministry of a traditional, conservative evangelical church. Rick Warren, the author of the bestselling *Purpose Driven Life*, who has some experience in growing a successful, large church, has said that if you attempt to change a traditional church into a progressive, renewed church, you will have tremendous difficulty and are setting yourself up to fail (see *The Purpose Driven Church* pages 179-180). Since most of the graduates of seminary and Bible college go to traditional, conservative evangelical churches and are eager to put into practice new ideas, new programs, and new structures, you can see that the potential for conflict and tension is great. I don't know if Jeffrey knew this, but like Matthew, he came in loaded for bear, so to speak, and began to shake things up right off the bat.

There was one difference between Jeffrey and Matthew in terms of the churches they were working in. Matthew had a board that was pretty mature, had wisdom and grace, and was willing to let Matthew do pretty much whatever he wanted, and even when Matthew blew up in that Wednesday night service, they let him remain as pastor and continued to work with him until he left. Jeffrey did not have this luxury when he came to the church. His board was pretty conservative and not as flexible or mature at the beginning, and Jeffrey knew this, and while he tried to go slow in some respects, he almost could not help himself and created some tension and problems for himself right from the beginning. Some people see any type of change as negative and have to be brought along slowly to accept the changes that the pastor might want to make. It takes time to get people to trust you, to take ownership of changes, and a lot of communication and teaching.

While Jeffrey did connect with the congregation on a personal level, it was unfortunate that his wife did not. She did not seem to share in his enthusiasm for coming to the church; I think she thought that Jeffrey would end up working at the seminary in some fashion, which would be like a "normal" job. Instead, she became a pastor's wife, a role for which she was not suited and in which she found no joy or happiness. In some ways, the role of a pastor's wife is more difficult than that of the pastor, unless she works outside of the home, which is much more common today than it was a generation ago. Some churches think that when they hire the pastor, the wife is hired as well. I have actually heard the phrase "two for the price of one" used by search committees who have valued the skills that the wife brings—skills such as playing the piano or organ, working with children or ladies, leading some type of small group, etc. It has taken about a generation for the church's attitude about pastors' wives to change from an unpaid minister in the church to a person in her own right who is not required to work in the church as an associate of some sort.

I liked Jeffrey and found him easy to converse with. He was interested in my wife and young child, and because we had both spent years studying the Bible in a formal setting, we shared an interest in all things biblical. It was at this time in my life that I began to read works by the Puritans, evangelical Christians who lived during the 1600s in England. Their works had a depth and spirituality about them that seemed to be missing in much of contemporary Christian literature, and over the course of a year, they would influence my thinking in a significant and lasting way. After about a year, Jeffrey proposed that I think about becoming a deacon at the church. I had been attending the church for about three years at this point, was leading the youth group, and was a Bible college graduate. He also proposed putting another man on the board, another seminary graduate who had come to the church when Jeffrey arrived. He and his wife were just beginning to look for a church to pastor, a search that would take almost a year. (This man would take a church in California and would have such a terrible experience that he would leave that church after a year or so and never go back into the ministry; instead he became a schoolteacher.)

To be asked to serve on the leadership board of a church was pretty heady stuff for a twenty-four-year-old; if I had any brains I would have said no. I was just too young and inexperienced. Jeffrey should have known that. Jeffrey thought (as would be proved by events in the future) that I could be a vote for whatever he wanted to do and might serve to counterbalance some of the more conservative guys on the board. After being on the board for a number of months, there came an issue before us that would cause my wife and me to leave the church, though we certainly did not see that coming and were very happy with the church's place in our lives.

In 1976, Campus Crusade for Christ launched a huge evangelistic campaign that was called "I Found It." The idea was to get churches to partner with Crusade in this effort that was designed to reach out to the friends and neighbors of church members. The campaign used billboards and bumper stickers with the phrase "I Found It" framed in yellow as a teaser. The hope was that people would wonder what on earth this was, and then when contacted by their friends and neighbors who happened to be Christians, they would be automatically interested in the message of the gospel. I had some real reservations about the whole thing when Jeffrey brought it before the board, hoping to get our approval so the church could participate in the campaign with other churches (eventually almost every evangelical church in the city would be involved, and the yellow bumper stickers and billboards became ubiquitous in the coming weeks). One night when my wife and I were watching the national news, we saw a story on the "I Found It" campaign, and it was quite upsetting. The man in charge of the national campaign, who worked for Campus Crusade, said on national TV, in reference to the use of bumper stickers and billboards, that in the first century of the church the apostles had to rely on the Holy Spirit, whereas today (1976) we had mass marketing available and could rely on that instead. Needless to say, we were not impressed.

One week or so prior to the board meeting to discuss this issue, Jeffrey gave me a book by Bill Bright (the founder and president of Campus Crusade) to read. He knew that I would read anything that he gave me, so I took home and put it on my desk. It was called *Come Help Change the World* and was a philosophical statement on the importance of world evangelism. For some reason, I did not get a chance to read the book before we met as a board to discuss participating in "I Found It," but it would not have really mattered if I had. I don't think that Jeffrey had to get permission from the board to be involved in the campaign, but he brought up the benefits of the church participating in it and wanted our approval. He went around the group to get our opinion and thoughts, starting with the man next to me, which meant that I would end up being the last to speak.

The other guys had no real objections. I think that Jeffrey knew that, and his hope was that I would be swayed by having everyone else on board (how he knew that I might have objections to the campaign was beyond me; my guess is that in his heart he too may have had some misgivings, and if he had them, then I might as well). You have to remember that I was only twenty-four years old; the other men on the board were on average twenty years older than I was. I hated conflict and only had a vague notion of why I did not want to be involved in the campaign. Still, when it came my turn, I expressed my reservations about something that to me was very much a tease, very impersonal, and relied on concepts centered on marketing strategies. Each man when they spoke voted to participate. I offered to just abstain from voting so Jeffrey could have a unanimous vote, but he would have none of it. He asked me for biblical reasons that I had for not wanting to participate. I told him that my main concern was that it seemed to be relying on methods and ideas that could have come out of the business world and that there must be better ways to reach people. He came after me for about twenty minutes, asking questions, mocking my answers, all the time walking around the room as he spoke. I didn't really come to the meeting thinking I would have to give a presentation on anything, so not only was I caught off guard, I felt personally attacked and humiliated by Jeffrey.

This was the first time in our lives that my wife and I had a bad experience at church, and we did not know how to feel or respond. There was a rather lame attempt to get us to come back to the church, but no one ever apologized to us; no one ever tried to get Jeffrey and me together to work things out, so we just got on with our lives. Over the years I have noticed that when people leave churches, many times there is little effort made to find out why, or if there have been problems or conflict, to try and reconcile those who have been involved. Those in church leadership seldom know either how to resolve conflict at the time or how to bring people back together later. To be honest, I really did not want to be reconciled. I felt I had done nothing wrong, and it felt good to be the "injured party" (pride, yet again). This confirmed to me that what I believed about the "I Found It" campaign was right, and a dark cloud of pride would follow me for a number or years as I felt that I had been forced to leave a church because I stood up for the truth. The truth was more complicated. I left because I had been hurt and did not know how to relate to another Christian (let alone a pastor) who had humiliated and attacked me because of something I said and believed.

As time went on and I got stronger emotionally (or more cynical about how churches work), that incident would not have prompted such a drastic reaction, but you live to the level of your maturity and life experience, and that was that. I ran across Jeffrey years later at the seminary (he ended up working at the seminary as his wife had perhaps wanted all along, but by this point their marriage was on its last legs and they would be divorced within a year), and we had a nice conversation about how each of us was doing—pretty shallow stuff, but sometimes it's okay to just talk about stuff. We were certainly not going to go back to the incident at church that was way in the past. One of my friends ran across Jeffrey a few years after that, and when my name came up, he mentioned that what he had done to me was wrong and that he regretted it. When I heard this, I was surprised. I would have thought that all those years later he would have pretty much forgotten about what had happened; so much water had gone under the bridge for him.

When you leave a church, you have two options: find another church to attend or just stop going to church. It was not an option for us to just stop going to church, so we thought about what to do. It is a growing problem in the evangelical world that many people have just stopped going to church yet still consider themselves devoted followers of Christ. I understand if you have been hurt by another Christian or had a bad experience at a church (church split, personality conflicts, etc.) that it can be difficult to get back into going to church, but many people choose not to attend church when they have not experienced either of the above. This phenomenon has been chronicled by George Barna in his book *Revolution* and shows no signs of slowing. Our hurt eventually went away as we got involved in another church, but lingering just below the surface there was a feeling that we were not aware of at the time, a feeling that we could not trust those who were in leadership in the church. Our experience with Matthew at our home church did not hurt us but I think it unconsciously left its mark, while Jeffrey's actions definitely left us a little less trusting of pastors, though I did not recognize it at the time.

## Principles for the Pastor

1.  *Developing leaders*. It is my hope that most pastors do not feel like they have to lead every meeting and teach every class. Unless the church is very small or a church plant, a pastor will have to rely on others to do much of the ministry of the church. Your concern should be twofold: to have those who minister do so with excellence, and for them to do so according to their gifts and temperament. Ministering with excellence is a standard that a pastor can promote and expect for their church. Expecting it is one thing; achieving it is another. Some pastors will inherit people who have worked for years in a particular ministry that is just not suited to their talents, personality, or abilities; it may be that they will have

to be removed from their position. If not removed, a pastor will be handicapped by allowing someone to serve who is the exception to a policy of maintaining excellence and serving according to gifting and ability.

2. *The job of pastor.* Being a pastor is a job, but it is more than that. Pastors get a salary; they usually have an office and perhaps a staff; they have goals, programs that they are responsible to run, as well as budgets and other financial matters. Yet in many ways, this job is unlike what we term *secular employment.* Pastors usually do not have set hours (though many of them wish they did), and their income is dependent on the goodwill of others.

There are two ways to look at being a pastor: as a job or as a ministry. There are those who view their positions mainly as a job and not as a ministry. The other side of this coin is that a pastor might become so invested in the work of the church and the lives of the people that it consumes him, to the detriment of his family and possibly his health and emotional well-being. As in many situations in life, the answer is found in maintaining a balance somewhere in the middle.

3. *How do you determine if you are called to the ministry?* Many others have written on this subject, but I have a few thoughts that I have acquired over the years. I felt called to the ministry as a young man (that is why I went to Bible college) but did not end up in "full-time ministry" until about thirty years later. Is "full-time ministry" the only type that is the result of a "call"? Listening to many pastors, you would think so. Being called to the ministry is different, they think, from God calling someone to some other type of job. They would say it is more spiritual, more sacrificial, and more distinctive to be called to the ministry. Men who are called to the ministry are ordained, set apart by the church, educated in special schools, and have more knowledge about the Bible than most lay people.

How men determine if they are called is another manner. I don't doubt that God leads and gifts men to be in the ministry; my problem is that our motives and desires may influence our decision to enter the ministry, and in a fallen world, motives and desires can be selfish and misunderstood. Most men who are called to the pastorate love to speak; preaching and teaching in front of others can lead to self-fulfillment and a confirmation of God's call to the ministry. But it may also indicate a desire to be noticed, to be admired, and to be in leadership over others. The fact that many men leave the ministry after only a few years may mean several things: they might not have been "called" to the ministry in the first place, they misread their gifting, or their training did not give them the ability to fulfill their calling.

4.  *How do churches pick the men who will serve as elders?* Churches have different ways to fill the position of elder. Some churches have search committees and some churches have the elder board nominate men to serve. The problem does not lie in the process used to find men to serve; the problem lies in the type of men who are chosen to be elders. Though there are two lists of qualifications for those who are to serve as elders (1 Tim. 3 and Titus 1), many men serve who are not qualified to be elders and bring harm to churches and pain and difficulty to the pastor. As pastor, your input on who is chosen to be on the board can run the spectrum of little to no input or personally choosing those who will serve. Usually the reality is somewhere in the middle. If a pastor does not want someone to serve, he can make this known to the committee or board, and if his reasons are valid, he will probably get his way.

The temptation is that a pastor may want men on the board who are not qualified but have influence in the church due to any number of reasons (large family following in the church, large giving, long-time member at the church). Since the composition of the board will determine to a significant extent his success in the church, he might be tempted to want those who agree with him philosophically or those with whom he has a good personal relationship. Please fight the temptation to put those on the board who might be easy to work with but are not qualified biblically. If a pastor only has on the board those who agree with him, he may try to manipulate them to get what he wants in terms of programs, structures, etc. Also, please stand up for the biblical qualifications in those who serve on your board and have the integrity to question those candidates who should not serve. This may be difficult and take courage, but that's what pastors have signed up for.

5. *How to recover from a bad church experience?* If a man remains in the ministry long enough, he will be hurt, misunderstood, his motives and character will be questioned, and he may even be betrayed and slandered. Most pastors think this will never happen to them until it actually does, and many leave the ministry because of how they are treated by their churches. I have talked to many pastors who have been ready to quit their churches over how they or their families have been treated. Many do quit and have negative feelings about the church for years and cannot find relief for the bitterness and hurt they experience.

So when this happens to you, what will you do? If you are able to stay at your church, you have to find it in your heart to forgive. This means you will get over your bitterness, you will get over your anger, and you will not continually have bad thoughts about those who have hurt you. God can do this work in your life if you let Him. He has done it in my life, and I hope you have not experienced the depth of hurt that I have from churches and church leaders. Second, you have to find a way to keep whatever person or situation that caused your hurt from happening again if that is possible. This will probably involve discussions with people who will be difficult and intensely personal, but this is what you have to do if you want to stay and minister to your church. It is easier to just stay secretly bitter and mad, but it will eat you up inside, and you cannot live that way for very long. Find someone you trust whom you can talk to about what you are feeling or have experienced; they might be able to also serve as a facilitator to reconcile you and whoever has caused you difficulty or hurt. You may have to leave your church, but don't just leave without trying to remedy the hurt; you will just take it with you to the next church. You may want to avoid the conflict that sometimes comes with trying to explain to another person how they have hurt you. I did that for years, and it got me only deeper into emotional denial. Get it out, get it out quickly, and get it over with. God will surprise you many times by bringing healing to a situation that you thought was irreconcilable.

# Questions to Ponder

## Developing Leaders

1. What is your current plan to develop leaders in your church?

2. Would your church members say that the programs and events in your church are done with excellence?

3. Do you set the tone for the church by maintaining excellence?

4. How do you deal with those who are not qualified to be in leadership?

## The Job of Pastor

1. How do you view your role as pastor in terms of job and/or ministry?

2. Do you leave your "job" at the church or bring it home with you?

3. Compared to your board members and their employment, how much more or less emotionally invested in your job as pastor are you?

4. How many hours a week do you work compared to your board members?

5. Would you prefer your congregation call you by your name or your title?

## Your Education

1. Be honest. Did your education at seminary or Bible School help you develop a more vital relationship with God? If yes, how can you help your church have that same experience through your ministry to them? If no, what might have been the reason?

2. Do you look on your congregation as basically unlearned in the Bible and your job to teach them what you know?

3. How much time do you spend in study each week? What do you think is appropriate?

4. How do you balance your knowledge of the Bible with humility, grace, and tact?

## Called to the Ministry

1. How did you experience God calling you to the ministry?

2. When you felt called to the pastorate, did you automatically feel you needed to go to seminary or Bible college?

3. Do you think you need to be "successful" to validate your call to the ministry?

4. Do you view your calling as something that sets you apart from your congregation in terms of occupation?

5. How much do you think speaking ability relates to being called to the pastorate?

6. Have others confirmed to you your calling to the ministry? Do you think this type of confirmation is important?

## Elders

1. Do you allow men to serve as elders who are not qualified? Do you always have a choice in the matter?

2. Does your church generally pick those who fit the profile of an elder found in 1 Timothy 3 and Titus 1?

3. What do with men who are elected to the board but eventually show they are not qualified?

## Bad Church Experiences

1. When was your last bad church experience? How did you feel? How did you respond? How did your family respond if they knew of the circumstance?

2. If there are still lingering effects from that experience, what are they? Are these effects hindering your ministry now?

3. Did you need to forgive someone for the way they acted? Have you done that?

4. Was your board involved? How did they react? Did it affect your relationship to the board?

5.  How do your normally deal with bad church experiences?

6.  How has God helped you get through this type of situation in your life?

7.  Can you see another bad experience coming? How might you either prepare for it or avoid it?

# The Big Church

So after talking together, my wife and I decided to attend the church that was associated with the Bible college that I had attended. We had been listening to the pastor on the radio Sunday evenings, and we liked what we heard. The pastor in his sermons quoted some of the authors I was reading, so this was a big plus in my mind. It was a big church, we had some friends there, and it was very close to where we lived. Although we never expressed the thought, I thought after being in two small churches, it might be good to just blend in for a while. Our family was growing. I was being promoted at my job. So one Sunday we showed up at the new church to see what it was like.

The church was started by the same man who had started the Bible college and had a long and storied history. The founder, Dr. Standish, was widely known in the evangelical world; he was wonderful preacher who spoke in an English accent and had a genuine love for people, especially the students who attended the Bible college, many of whom considered him to be their spiritual father. He had given up being pastor of the church about ten years previously (he was about seventy at this time) and turned it over to his associate. It is a difficult thing to follow someone who is famous, has a distinctive preaching style, and almost has a personality cult. The church had declined since Dr. Standish had left, not unusual in itself but a potential breeding ground for unhappiness with the current pastor.

The pastor's name was David; he was in his late forties when we arrived. He was a decent, kind, gentle, and humble man who had no clue how to be a pastor. I know this sounds critical, but it is true. He would have done much better as a professor at a seminary or Bible college; as a pastor he was way out of his depth and giftedness. Whereas Dr. Standish had a large personal following when he was pastor, David had little personal following; he was merely the pastor. Like many influential churches, this one was living largely on its history as the biggest, most prominent evangelical church in the city for almost thirty years, though those days were long gone. David spent nearly all of his time in study; he rarely left the office except for hospital visits to the growing number of elderly people who had been at the church for decades. He felt that preaching was his primary calling and did not realize that he was losing the people because he was not connecting with them on a personal level.

Because he came from an era when many mainline denominations had retreated from orthodox Christianity into liberalism, his ministry context was to teach and preach the Bible to this flock as the inspired Word of God. He thought of spiritual growth in terms of knowing more of the Bible, and though his sermons did have some application in them, because he had never worked in the "real world" they did not really resonate with people. Still, I thought he was a great teacher, and it was from David that I first heard someone preach Reformed or Calvinistic doctrine. He was careful to never use the words *Calvin* or *Calvinism*; he knew that there was a difference of opinion among the congregation (many of whom either worked or taught at the Bible college), but he was not afraid to teach on election, predestination, the sovereignty of God, and the sinfulness of man, since these words and concepts were found in many places in the Bible.

He came to believe in the system of Calvinism later in his life, so those who were a little more knowledgeable about the Bible did sense a shift in emphasis in his preaching, and the whispering began. It is a testament to his character that though he knew this was going on, he did not change how he preached or try to appease his board, some of whom were beginning to question him about what he believed. The problem was that the Bible college and the seminary that he had graduated from were not quite as Calvinistic as David was, and some on the board thought that they could use this against him, claiming that he was changing what he believed. While this was true, there really wasn't that much difference in what David believed and taught and what the Bible college (and Dr. Standish) believed and taught. The main difference in his theological position was that as a committed Calvinist he believed in what is termed *limited atonement,* that Christ died only for the church. Though he never taught this from the pulpit, those in the know knew he believed this because he was a Calvinist, and they did not want someone as their pastor who believed that Jesus did not die for everyone. This point has been debated endlessly by those in the evangelical world and is held by most of those in Reformed denominations, but for those who have never been exposed to the intricacies of theological debate, just saying that Jesus did not die for everyone can seem like heresy—that is, until you begin to look at what the Bible has to say on the subject; then it isn't quite so easy to dismiss the view that Christ only died for the church.

I believe that those on the board who thought the church was going downhill could affect a change in leadership if they labeled David as Calvinistic, as if that were something terrible. Because David was not the most outgoing person in the world, to call him a Calvinist made him seem more cold and remote and less interested in reaching people with the gospel. Once someone has been tagged with a label, whatever it is, they are given all of the baggage that goes with that label, whether it is true of them or not. Labeling people is not necessarily a bad thing; the problem is that everyone has a different interpretation of the word used as a label. If you want to label me as a Christian, that's great because it is true. If you label me as a *fundamentalist,* that may also be true, but that word in our culture has a lot of negative meaning associated with it. So David got labeled by some in the church as a Calvinist, and he couldn't escape the negative connotations that some associate with that word.

I did not know that any of this was going on at the time; I was too busy enjoying our time there. We especially liked going on Wednesday night. There was a dinner before the Bible class we attended, and we got to know a lot of the people who belonged to the church. David always ate with his extended family. He had two grown sons who attended the church, one of whom was the associate pastor. If he had been more of a people person, he might have had dinner with a different group of people each week, but as I have said, he just did not get that as pastor he really needed to connect and relate to those he led. After the dinner, there was a program for the kids that was run with great enthusiasm and professionalism, and our little kids looked forward to it each week. All in all, it was a great experience, one that we still look back on with affection. It felt normal to go to that church because it was pretty big; we were not aware of what was going on behind the scenes, the dark clouds on the horizon that would result in the church splitting and David resigning as the pastor.

Churches split for any number of reasons. Most splits are a long time coming; they involve issues that have been simmering below the surface for a while and are triggered by some incident that is either planned (a vote of confidence on the pastor, for example) or happens spontaneously. All church splits are messy, but those that happen spontaneously can be devastating; all of the pent-up emotions, feelings, and attitudes come right to the surface, leaving no time to either talk things through or prepare for what is coming. Some churches split over things that involve money, some over personality issues (this usually means someone is not getting what they want, perhaps a influential member of the congregation or a board member who thinks they know more than the pastor), some over a specific issue on which there are two opposing sides, and some over a specific doctrinal issue, though this is somewhat rare. Because churches many times cannot see the split coming, there is seldom an attempt to get whatever issue is causing the division dealt with before it erupts into a fissure. Most of this fault can be traced back to the pastor and the board and the failure to deal with issues that have the potential to split the church. Seldom do those in leadership have meetings with the congregation to discuss the problems that can lead to a split, so those who have different opinions or hurt feelings or bad attitudes do not have the occasion to talk about what they are experiencing. It does take a great deal of wisdom and tact to lead these types of meetings, but the alternative is much worse. By doing nothing, you allow people to continue in behaviors that can wreck a church. David knew that there was talk going on about him, but he chose to take the high road and stay above the fray, as it were, instead of letting people have the opportunity to talk to him about their concerns and opinion of where the church was headed. This might not have changed the situation, but it would have shown that he knew what was going on and was not above letting people talk to him in a public setting instead of talking to others in one of the hallways of the church after the service or on the telephone late at night.

Churches also split because the expectations of one group or another are not being met. Everyone who attends church has some expectation of what that experience will be like, and when those expectations are not met, there can be trouble. It is not unusual for some Christians to equate their spiritual lives with how they feel about church and what they experience when they attend. If their experience is good and they feel positive about church, then they feel good about their relationship with God and are generally happy with their lives. If their church experience is not what they want it to be, then they find it hard to be satisfied with their Christian life. This is a big burden for a pastor to bear, because he is the one that most church members feel is responsible for making the church a place where they have a good spiritual experience, and because the church has such a diverse group of people attending, it can be almost impossible to structure and organize a church where everyone is happy with the music, programs, and philosophy.

The problem with all of this is that Christians should not come to church with the attitude of what they can get or how they are going to feel, but rather what can they give, who can they minister to, where can they minister, etc. Not only do people have expectations of what they will experience in church, they also have expectations of how the church should look, and without exception, most of those who attend evangelical churches feel that their churches should look bigger, not smaller. When a church goes into decline, some in the church seem to take this personally, and if there is no turnaround, something is going to give, and usually that will be the pastor.

David could see that the church was declining but took no steps in terms of new programs, strategies, outreach, or anything else to try and turn the tide. It is a sad but true fact that one of the main reasons that churches grow is the personality and preaching of the pastor. If the pastor preaches sermons that are stimulating, relational, and have applications that hit people "where they live," then it is possible to attract large numbers of new people (this is what had happened under Dr. Standish). The quickest way to turn a church around numerically is to bring in a new pastor who is a great communicator and whose messages have a way of connecting with people. Adding large numbers of new people says nothing about the health of a church, and most of the time these new people are already Christians, but any church that is growing numerically is considered a success.

It is interesting that one of the most influential churches in America, Willow Creek Church in Chicago, Illinois, recently surveyed the thousands of people who attend and found that though they have grown dramatically since their founding, they have failed to mature their membership, a rare admission of failure on the part of a church that most people would consider to be quite successful. They wrote a book about this called *Reveal*.

David was a good preacher, but he was not the type who could bring lots of new people to the church. The new Calvinistic emphasis in his preaching, and the resulting criticism that was beginning to surface on this issue, probably contributed to a bunker mentality that made it impossible to try anything different to reinvigorate the church—not that he would have known what to do anyway. He only had about half of his board with him at this point, and it is doubtful that he could have gotten them to go in a different direction had he wanted to.

Church boards come in many shapes and sizes; the board at this church was called the *church council* and had twenty members. It was a holdover from when Dr. Standish had been the pastor; by this time, it had too many members, some of whom had been on the board for twenty or more years. One of the board members was a self-made man who owned a very profitable business and was not above criticizing the pastor to anyone who would listen. He knew how to do this in a backhanded manner, without being too obvious, but his intention to get the pastor to quit or be replaced was pretty transparent to those in the know. I knew this man on a casual basis because before I was married I had house-sat for him when he and his wife went on vacation. I would have never known he was a schemer, someone who did not deal in the open but in the shadows; he was very pleasant to me, though I did notice that his wife never smiled. Not once did she ever display any happiness in any encounter I had over the years with her.

David and his son (the associate pastor) and two other church council members were aware of this man's attempts to divide the board and the church and finally got the courage to go to talk with him about this. The day they set aside to do this, the man's mother died, and circumstances would prevent them from ever having that conversation, though it probably would not have mattered if they did. Years later it would be revealed that the man had a long-time mistress; he lost his wife, his position at the church, his testimony (which admittedly wasn't much), his business and son over his adultery, and he died a few years later a sad and lonely man. I have watched with interest how churches choose their leaders; those men who serve as elders, deacons, or church council members will determine with the pastor the success or failure of the church.

Although it is never said out loud, many churches put men on their boards who have lots of money and have been successful in business. There is no better way to get rich people to give to the church than to involve them in the decision-making process and give them a sense of ownership regarding the direction of the church. All churches seek to have elders who are spiritual, but in my experience, few churches ask a candidate about his spiritual journey, his family, or his testimony at work.

It is assumed that if you attend church regularly with your family and have no obvious sins, then you must be doing well spiritually. Church attendance is one of the key factors; if you make all of the meetings of the church, it is assumed that your support of the church means that you will make a good leader. Churches seldom ask elders what their philosophy of ministry is, what they think about current issues in the evangelical world (things like open theism, egalitarianism, women in ministry, etc.), or what Christian books they have read lately. I have known elders who have never read a book by a Christian author but can name the staring lineup of the Atlanta Braves from the 1990s. Yet it is these men who are responsible for the doctrinal purity of the church and keeping the church free from heresy. But really, since the pastor has gone to seminary and knows all that stuff, that responsibility can be given to him; that's what we pay him for.

But that was in the future. I don't know what the exact circumstances were that brought the church council together to have a confidence vote on the pastor. Churches are governed in some respects by their documents, usually a church constitution and some sort of bylaws. Most states require churches to have these documents in order to be a tax-exempt corporation; these documents can be the guiding instrument in how to chose and then get rid of a pastor. Most church bylaws give the board some kind of power to dismiss a pastor, but the reality is that if the pastor does not have the board with him, they can merely have a vote of no confidence no matter what the bylaws may say, and the pastor will then usually resign; no man is going to serve with a board that has no trust or confidence in him. So the church board got together to discuss the situation, and in the course of this meeting, a confidence vote was taken. The vote was eleven to nine; it really did not matter at that point whether the eleven were for David or against; you cannot serve as the pastor of a church with half of the board opposed to you (eleven were opposed to David, as it turned out).

Though the vote was framed in terms of David's doctrinal position, the real issue was that David was not Dr. Standish, and the church had been in a steady decline for years, and David had done nothing to try and halt that decline. Both David and the board probably did not realize that every church has a life cycle, from birth to death, and that this church was on the way down toward death; having been in existence for about forty years at that point, it had passed through infancy to adolescence to maturity and then was headed toward old age and then death. Every church, group, or organization goes through a cycle like this and will eventually need to reinvent itself with a new vision or purpose to continue, or it will cease to grow and eventually die or become irrelevant. David could not bring that vision to the church, so it continued to decline; this is what I believe caused the vote of no confidence.

David preached once more, the following Sunday. Most of the congregation, myself included, had no idea of what had happened. The service went on like normal; when David got up to preach, few knew that it would be his last sermon in that church. He was the epitome of grace and humility in how he spoke; though because he knew this was his last Sunday, he seemed to me to be a little more forceful and passionate than usual. He told the church that he would be leaving because he had lost most of the board (he did not mention the eleven to nine number) over his teaching of what he called "the doctrines of grace." He pointed out that while he was being voted out, so to speak, for being a Calvinist, he had never used that word or quoted from Calvin himself and regretted the furor that he had caused by just preaching what he understood the Bible to mean. He did not say anything about starting another church, nothing about his own future, and nothing about the future of the church. Normally when he was done preaching he walked to the front of the church during the last song to greet people as they left; this Sunday he left without talking to anyone so as not to be the center of attention. What this cost him personally he never revealed, but you know that it must have wounded him deeply. No one could ever accuse him of any sin; he never got angry, never lost his temper, and was never petulant or self-centered. Those on the board (and in the church) who wanted him gone had only his supposed doctrinal difference to force him out. To my knowledge, no one ever brought up the fact that the church was declining, which would have happened in most churches. At any rate, he was gone, and that was that.

I don't know if David ever thought about what the consequences of what he was going to do were going to be. If he started another church, he would split the old church and further reduce its numbers, though it was certain that a lot of people were going to leave because they would not want to be led by a church council that had no confidence in a pastor they admired. There was some doubt that he could have found another church to pastor—the difficulty of being a Calvinist who was not a Presbyterian limited the kinds of churches he might apply to. There weren't many Reformed Independent Baptist-type churches out there; besides, he had lived in the city his whole life, most of his kids and grandkids lived there, and I bet there might have been a part of him that felt if people wanted him to be their pastor, then he was going to be their pastor, even if it meant starting another church in the same town.

The first meeting of what would become a new church was held the following Sunday in a high school auditorium. There was a real air of excitement; everyone was looking around to see who had decided (at least at that point) to leave the old church and support David in whatever this was going to become. I know that some came to the service so that they could report back to the church council what David was up to and who had left, but that was probably to be expected. The service was actually pretty normal. David did not go around high-fiving everyone; he was pretty matter of fact and businesslike, not wanting to raise anyone's expectations because he did not know what the future was going to hold.

There were about three to four hundred people at that first service, which was about one-third of the old church. It would settle at around 250 after about a month, not bad for a new church.

It began life with a solid financial base, doctrinal unity, a positive attitude among those in the congregation, and many gifted people capable of doing all kinds of ministry (most of the people who had been doing the bulk of the volunteer ministry at the old church came to the new church, which made one wonder how the old church functioned those first few months). The church moved around those first few months, looking for a more permanent location, and finally settled on a vacant school property that had plenty of room. We met in what had been the cafeteria; it was not the greatest place to preach, but it was adequate. There was an adult Sunday school taught by the pastor's son and another man, children's Sunday school, and a class for the youth. Eventually the church voted in some elders (as opposed to *church council* members, this church chose the biblical name for its leaders); most of these men had been on the church council at the old church, all were chosen by David, nearly all of them were successful white-collar businessmen, and most were self-employed. I had secretly hoped that I might be one of the elders, but it was not to be, and for good reason. I had written David a twenty-five-page treatise containing principles that might be helpful for us as a new church; my guess is that he found it a little too nontraditional. I was still pretty idealistic at this time and thought that he would be interested in what I had to say, but he never gave me an indication that he had ever read it.

I really wanted the church to work for us. I really did. After all, our experience at the old church had been great, I was a confirmed Calvinist myself, and I greatly respected David. But as the months went on and the church settled into a pattern, it became obvious that there was not going to be anything for me to do. I wanted to teach again, but there was no opportunity to do so. The only people who had a chance to minister were those on the elder board or David's sons. I can understand this after the experience he had had, but this just left most of us just sitting in chairs each Sunday. The church had no small groups, just one adult Sunday school class (it averaged about ninety people so you could have broken it down into classes based on age, season of life, or electives, but this never happened). The class had no interaction at all; it was just basically a forty-five-minute teacher-driven lesson, another opportunity to learn more information about the Bible.

I decided to go talk to David about my situation to see if there might be something that I could do at the church. I had spent five years getting a degree in theology and had experience teaching and felt that I could contribute to the church in some manner, even if it wasn't doing some type of teaching. We met at his house, the church did not have any offices at this point, and I explained my dilemma to him. He was very understanding and kind, but he was not moved by my situation. He said that there wasn't always something for everyone to do in churches and gave me no indication that there would ever be anything for me to do. When I brought up the fact that the other churches that I had been involved in had been much smaller and had all kinds of ministries for people to be involved in, he merely shrugged. Most pastors would be thrilled to have people come to them offering to help in the ministry of the church; in most churches, the ministries are done by 20 percent of the members, some having more than one position because there just are not enough people to fill the positions in the church. This can lead to burnout and frustration for those who do all of the work; that's why most pastors and leaders would never turn anyone away from serving who is even remotely qualified. The real issue here was that David and the other leaders did not want the church to have a lot of programs or ministries; they felt their main job was to teach the Bible, which could be done by a few men. I am sure that the experience of being forced out of a church because of what he taught and believed had an influence on how David and the board set up the structure of the church, which left me with nothing to do. He did tell me that he would talk to the elders about my situation and then get back to me, which left me with a little hope. After six weeks, I had heard nothing and decided that nothing was going to change.

So here I was, a young Bible college graduate who was itching to do something with all of that education, who had spent several years teaching kids on a weekly basis, and was told by a man that I really admired that there was nothing for me to do. It had only been a few years since we had left the Baptist church. Was I going to do that again? People leave churches for many reasons—hurt feelings, inability to get along with someone, difference over the direction of the church, not being able to relate to the current pastor, wanting a better kids' program. We just had someone leave my current church because there were not any marriage prospects. I guess they had never heard of eHarmony or Match.com. But few people leave because they are told that there is no place for them to minister. I mean, it wasn't like I wanted to preach every other week. I didn't ask for any specific position, just something to do.

My wife and I talked it over; to leave the church meant starting over again in another church, getting to know people, having them get to know us, and then hoping that there would be something that I could do, preferably in a teaching role. Most churches do not let new people into teaching roles until they have a chance to get to know them. For evangelical churches, teaching the Bible is a sacred trust; most do not let just anyone assume a teaching position, even if they have graduated from a seminary or Bible college. One of the other factors that figures into people leaving churches is the strength of the relationships that they have in the church. If you have lots of friends or family members, it can be extremely difficult to just up and leave. You will still see these people, and it can take time for those relationships to get back to some kind of normal. We had friends at the church, but most of my close friends had attended Bible college with me and had either left the city for further education or gone to other churches. All of our family was in California, so that was not a problem. We figured that we could make new friends; it just was not going to be worth it going to a church where I had no possibility to minister. Besides, we were busy raising young children who took up nearly all of our time. The church had no real children's ministry;

they just went through the motions, and so we thought it might be better for the kids if we attended a church that had a full-blown kids' department.

Depending on the circumstances involved, the leadership reacts in different ways when someone leaves their church. Sometimes they just don't care, there is no effort made to try and find out why, and there is no effort made to try and solve or identify whatever problem or circumstance made them leave. The size of the church also plays into how leadership may deal with those who have chosen to leave. If you are attending a large church and are only slightly or marginally involved, then when you leave, the odds are you are out free and clear. Large churches have people coming and going all the time; it takes someone who has either a following of some sort (maybe a large family attending the same church), is in a position of leadership, or gives a lot of money to rate a visit from the leadership to find out why they are leaving. Most of the time when people who are deeply involved in churches leave, the reason is known before they leave, and there may even have been attempts to either keep them at the church or find out why they have chosen to move on. In a small church, anyone who leaves is noticed and will usually start some sort of discussion among the membership: Did you notice that Paul and Sally have left?

It is much more common for the leadership of a small church to try and hold on to every member they can; just like in business, it costs more to get a new customer than to hold on to an existing one. When you lose a person or family who has attended your church for long time, you not only lose whatever skills and gifts they possessed, but you lose the dynamic they had in the church in terms of the other families and persons that they related to, and of course you lose their money. If a family leaves a small church where they were major givers, the resulting loss of income can affect everything the church does, especially if they take others with them, which is not uncommon. I was on a search committee in one church where a candidate wanted to know how many people gave over a certain amount of money per year; he was trying to find out if the budget was supported to a large extent by a few individuals. He knew he might lose some people if he was called and wanted to know if the church would be able to support him if he lost a major giver.

When we left the church, we did so without telling anyone. Because I had gone and talked with David about finding something in the church to do and was told that there might never be anything I could do, they knew that after two or three weeks something was up, and two of the elders called to see if they could come by and talk with us. They did not mention why they wanted to come by, but I think it was obvious. I knew both of these men, and when they came by, I was pretty relaxed because I had gone to the pastor with good intentions and was told that my role in the church was to just show up and sit, which was not in line with my view of how a church should function, nor did it allow me to use the gifts that God had given me for the benefit of the body. So I had a pretty clear conscience and felt no guilt or had any bad feelings about leaving. They were polite enough, but they had not talked to David about my conversation with him about wanting to serve in the church in any capacity that might be available, so they came with a whole different agenda. They focused on the fact that what I had done was wrong in that I was not being obedient to the leadership by just up and leaving. I told them that I did not just up and leave but had talked with David, who had promised to get back to me to see if there was some ministry that I could be involved in. I told them that I had waited six weeks and then had given up; I figured nothing was going to change, and I wanted to get on with my life. I asked them how they would feel if they did not have any opportunity to minister in the church but came and sat week after week.

During our meeting, I just sang the same song. I wanted to something to do, went to David to see if that was possible, was told that it was not possible but that he would get back to me, he did not get back to me, and what was I supposed to do? Apparently what I was supposed to do was go back to the church and be a good boy and stop causing problems. Everyone was very polite. There was no way to resolve the situation, but they gave it a good try.

You can try to manipulate people by using guilt, but it works best when the person you are trying to control either has done something wrong or has a weak will or low self-esteem. They were not going to get anywhere with me because I had tried to do the right thing by going to David. I did not leave trying to cause any hard feelings or dissension, and finally, I repeatedly pointed out to them from the Bible that the church is a body where everyone has a place to function, but they just did not get this and kept coming back to the obey-your-leaders part and came really close to telling me that I was sinning by leaving the church. That made me a little testy, but I wanted to keep the moral high ground, and I let that pass. So that was it; we had left our second church. (The New Testament is clear that church members should obey their leaders, but I doubt the command is absolute. You would not obey a leader who might lead you into sin or heresy, for example.)

As I have mentioned previously, one of the basic features of my personality is that I dislike conflict and disharmony, whether it is in the family, church, or workplace. In a few years, I would have my own small business and employ about fifteen people, and occasionally I had to let people go because of their performance. I hated this and usually held on to people much longer than I should have, always hoping that they would improve, and I would not have to confront and then dismiss them. One time I fired a long-time employee by leaving a note in their box and then leaving for vacation the next day so I would not have to face them. By nature, I will always avoid conflict. I am sure a psychiatrist could find something in my past that has made me into that kind of person.

Avoiding conflict is, of course, not always a good thing. You can let situations or circumstances in life get much more out of control or complicated than they need to be by letting things slide because you are afraid that by dealing with a situation people will get upset or there will be misunderstanding or hurt feelings. So I always approached situations that might produce conflict or hurt with real dread. Like most people, I wanted to be liked, and it is hard to have people like you when you are telling them you are leaving the church that they lead. I would run into people from the church from time to time over the years, and because God is good, there were no residual hard feelings or damaged relationships; everyone just got on with their lives. One of the elders even became my doctor for a time. You don't give someone that kind of control over your life if you don't trust and respect them.

## Principles for the Pastor

1. *Following in the footsteps of another pastor.* Unless you have started the church in which you serve, somebody was pastor at the church before you. Pastors have different practices regarding the previous man when they come to a church; some contact the pastor to find out as much as they can about the circumstances under which he left. Some pastors are diplomatic, talking around the edges, wanting the dirt that may be there so they do not go into their new ministry totally cold. Some pastors do not want to know anything about the former pastor, either because they fear what they may hear or figure whatever happened before is not relevant to them. Believe me, what the former pastor did, how he left, what the people think of him, all of these things will affect the ministry in a new church. The best source of information is probably the former pastor. I have found that most of them are pretty forthcoming without being slanderous on why they left and what a new pastor will find. There are people in the church who will volunteer information on the former pastor, but it will take time to know the context from which people in the church speak about him. The best thing a pastor can do is realize the former pastor left a mark on the church but not obsess about it.

2. *Developing empathy with those in your church.* Beyond being a pastor who can relate to those they minister to, there is the added measure of having empathy. Every pastor will have those in the church who hurt and have difficult personal situations (family issues, health issues, work issues, personal issues). These people will come for help, counsel, and encouragement. I think most people know that pastors will not be able to solve all of their dilemmas; many times they just need someone to listen, provide some counsel that is timely, and pray with them. Most of all, people want to know that pastors care about them and that when they hurt, you hurt. Few of us are good listeners, but pastors can learn to become people who listen as much as they talk. It is easier to empathize with someone if you yourself have faced suffering and difficulty in your life—easier, but not necessary.

There are two things that every pastor can do to show his congregation that he feels for them when they are in difficulty—listen and pray. Pastors may be able to offer advice, counsel, or wisdom that can bring healing and hope or a practical solution to a pressing problem, but sometimes they will not know what to say or how to help. That's okay. What pastors can say is that you know life is difficult but that Jesus is able to provide hope and strengthen their hearts, something that pastors cannot do. Pastors can promise to pray, check in, and perhaps find others to help in areas where they are not able.

Empathizing with people requires one more thing: time. If you have a short attention span and find your mind wandering as people are sharing their lives with you, you are not being sympathetic; you are just taking up space. Being a pastor requires you not only be able to teach, preach, and lead but also sympathize and relate to the difficulties your congregation will face. If you cannot be that kind of person, you are not being fair to those God has placed in your charge.

3. *Church splits.* Church splits come in all shapes and sizes, they are almost always messy and hurt the cause of Christ. Few church splits happen spontaneously; most are the result of circumstances that have been in place for some period of time and could have been foreseen if someone was looking. Which leads me to conclude that one of the reasons churches split is because the cause of the split is not dealt with before it becomes impossible to fix. Most church splits involve some type of conflict between individuals or groups over some issue or personality that has polarized people. Some pastors have seen a split coming but did not try to remedy the situation by getting people together to talk about whatever the issue was. Some pastors might have actually wanted the church to split (assuming they would be on the side that stayed at the church) so they could start over, as it were. The reality is, however, that most pastors are devastated by church splits. It destroys or sets back a pastor's ministry, some may have to leave a church and seek another opportunity, and it can wreck a family for years to come. What are the causes of church splits?

   a. **People want either power or influence that they do not currently have.** This puts pastors in the sights of those who want what they have. If pastors have people in their churches like this, they can do one of two things: make them their friends and ask for their advice and counsel regarding the affairs of the church or keep an eye on them and talk to them if their behavior becomes sinful (gossiping, slander, anger, disharmony, causing division). Pastors may have to involve their boards in talking to people like this, assuming they aren't on the board in the first place. Above all, spend time praying with those who may cause harm to the church

b. **Doctrinal differences.** This was the reason the big church I attended split, though I believe there were other factors involved. This type of split is less common and can be harder to resolve; people usually become fixed on their position and are not open to different interpretations or living graciously in disagreement. If a pastor sees this coming, they can begin to dialogue with people and perhaps keep the disagreement from becoming personal. Too many church splits happen in the hallways of the church and on the telephone.

c. **The church becomes too important.** Many Christians find too much of their identity and meaning in what happens at church. Church becomes the focus of their lives, not Christ, and since the church is at the center of their existence, everything that happens there these people have an opinion on. If they do not get their way on something (programs, building, structures, staff), they may try and get their way by forcing a pastor out, which many times causes the church to split. These people usually have some type of influence or power in the church.

d. **I am of Paul; I am of Peter; I am of Christ.** Every church has its own distinct groups and dynamics. These groups usually form according to stage of life or by age, but sometimes groups form because of issues or dissatisfaction. If a pastor is paying attention, they will know it when groups like this form and will work to keep the unity of the church by addressing the issues these people have. Many church splits could have been avoided if the pastor let people air their concerns and issues with the leadership. Some people just want to have their voices heard; they instinctively know they will not get what they want but do not want to be marginalized by not having anyone care about their opinion. Pastors may fear meeting with these people or groups like this. Better that pastors fear what might happen if they do not meet with them; they might be looking for a new church in the future.

4.  *The fastest way to grow a church.* It has been well documented that the fastest way to grow a church is to bring in a new pastor who is an exceptional speaker. I know that every pastor considers himself a great speaker; teaching and preaching are the two things that pastors usually find the greatest satisfaction in doing. People are drawn to those who can communicate well, and when a church brings in a new pastor who is a dynamic speaker and able to connect to his audience, churches can grow very quickly. It is hard to teach someone how to be a great speaker; it seems to be something that some men have and some men do not, a combination of background, education, personality, genes, and perhaps the right timing and situation.

    You probably know by this time in your life if you are one of those who can devise and deliver great sermons that will bring people to your church specifically to listen to you. If so, that's great; use that gift to mature those in your church by having programs and structures that will move them along in their spiritual journey. I hate to break this to you, but your preaching will not mature those who listen; your members need to be in relationships that will help disciple them. How do I know that your preaching will not make your members mature in Christ? It's because that is not the model that Jesus left us. He spent three years with the disciples, teaching with them, praying with them, doing ministry with them, and after those three years, they were ready to change the world. Your preaching provides vision, instruction, encouragement, information, and hope but was not intended to be the only way to grow people in Christ. If you can bring them in by your speaking ability, use that gift that you have been given, but realize it is only a part of how you make disciples of your congregation.

5. *The Pastor and the Board: Part Two.* I am specifically thinking here of those board members who cause pastors sleepless nights. It seems that every pastor will have a board member who is difficult to work with, one who thinks they know more than the pastor, one who seeks to impose his will and be the real leader or power in the church. Pastors may inherit them when they arrive, the congregation may want them on the board (either knowing or not knowing what they are like), or pastors might actually want them on the board to at least know what they are up to (keep your friends close and your enemies closer, so to speak). Regardless, pastors have to find a way to work with those who might be prone to selfishness, have power or control issues, seek to have undue influence over the direction of the church, or just be generally difficult to get along with. Since a pastor's relationship with the board will in large measure determine his success or failure in the church, and the odds are that every pastor will have board members who are difficult to work with, here are some guidelines to help with these type of men.

   a. Establish from the beginning how the board will function. If the members of the board can agree on how the board will work together, a pastor might be able to keep the members together as a unit and not allow one person to dominate the group.

   b. If one member is going to be a problem, make it a point to develop a relationship with that person outside of the group. Pastors may not want to do this (who wants to spend time with those who cause trouble?), but it will help the man see the pastor in another context.

c. Get other board members to help with those who are behaving badly. Since most board members who cause difficulty focus on the pastor, by having another board member talk with or confront, if necessary, the board member who is causing problems, it shows solidarity with the pastor and tends to isolate the misbehaving board member, hopefully helping him see he is a minority of one.

d. It might become necessary for a pastor to talk personally to a board member who is acting badly. Please make sure that the board member is actually behaving badly; if a board member disagrees with a pastor's vision, that does not necessarily mean he is being difficult. Most boards will not be unanimous in every situation or circumstance.

e. Spend time in board meetings praying for each other. Board meetings should not just be about church business, though my experience has been that those board members who want to just talk business are the ones who generally cause the most problems.

6. *Why pastors resign from churches.* Most pastors, if the statistics are to be believed, will resign from a church at least once in their life. Sometimes it is necessary, sometimes it is unavoidable, sometimes it happens quickly, and sometimes it happens over time. Each situation is different. There are some common themes on why pastors resign from churches.

a. Pastors might resign because they just cannot work with the board. We have already dealt with this at some length. You can only beat your head against a wall for so long; if the wall does not move or change, you just have to stop beating your head against it.

b.  Their family is falling apart because of the hours or the stress a pastor brings home from the church. If a pastor needs to work so much that it is causing his family to implode (especially his wife), either work fewer hours or find another job. The odds are if a pastor you are working so many hours that his family is complaining and missing him (if a pastor is working long hours and they are not missing him, that is another problem), his ministry is pretty much ineffective anyway; better to either get help from the board to fix his schedule or resign and save his family.

c.  They resign because they know they are either going to be fired or will be fired in the future. This, of course, brings up the question of why they might be getting the ax; I assume you are leaving because it has become impossible to work out whatever difficulties require you to look for something else.

d.  They resign because they have had unrealistic expectations regarding what being a pastor would be like. This is more common among those who are younger and have found that being a pastor was not what they signed up for; they grow discourage and quit, seldom to return to the ministry. Being a pastor is difficult, but just because something is difficult does not mean that you give up. Paul did not give up; read 2 Corinthians 11 again and see what he endured. If a man's expectation was that he would be the next Bill Hybels or Rick Warren, and the reality is that he is the pastor of a church of one hundred in the middle of the Texas panhandle, he might live in a state of constant disappointment and discouragement.

God is bigger than our reality, if we are where He wants us. Man up, and serve Him with grace and humility.

# Questions to Ponder

## Following in the Footsteps of Another Pastor

1. What does your congregation think of their former pastor?

2. What effects of the former pastor's ministry are still visible in the church? Did his manner of leaving affect your coming?

3. Have you talked to the former pastor? Was it profitable? Has the pastor who took over your old church talked to you?

4. How did or will you deal with the former pastor in the candidating process? What would you want to know?

## Developing Empathy for Those in Your Church

1. How well do you think you can help those who come to you in difficult circumstances?

2. What success or failures have you had in terms of dealing personally with people?

3. Do you find it easier to deal with Christians or non-Christians?

4. What are the circumstances under which you would refer someone to a professional counselor?

5. How do you safeguard yourself when you counsel those in difficulty with suffering, sins, or other issues?

6. Does you church sense that you are a sympathetic person? If not, why?

## Church Splits

1. Do you see a church split in your future in your current situation?

2. If you have been through a church split, how did it affect your view of:

   a. your church

   b. your board

   c. God

   d. the pastorate

3. How did your family respond? How did your wife deal with the split? Did it affect your relationship with her? If so, how did you repair it?

4. How did this experience affect your relationship with God? How did He help you through get through the experience?

5. Knowing that hindsight is 20/20, is there anything you would have done differently that might have prevented the church from splitting?

## The Fastest Way to Grow a Church

1. How would you rate your speaking ability on a scale of 1 to 10, 1 being putting those who come to hear you to sleep on a regular basis and 10 being the rebirth of Charles Spurgeon?

2. Do you think there are things you can do to improve as a speaker?

3. How much does empathy, compassion, and urgency relate to speaking ability?

4. How much do you pray before you speak? Have you asked God to make you a better communicator? Is God concerned about *how* you speak, not just what you speak?

5. On a scale of 1 to 10, how do you think your church would rate your speaking ability?

6. What do new people say about your messages and your ability as a communicator?

## The Pastor and the Board: Part Two

1. Do you have board members who behave badly during the meetings?

2. Why do you think they may act this way? Have you talked to them personally about their behavior?

3. Do other board members realize this type of bad behavior? Does it bother them?

4. Do you look at your board as a team? Have you tried to develop the board into a team?

5. Do you spend time with board members outside of the scheduled meetings?

6. In your meetings, do you pray for each other? Do you share personal details of your lives? Do you ever have elder retreats to discuss vision, goals, plans, and strategy?

7. How does your board deal with disagreement? Do you find ways to resolve it during the meetings?

## Resigning from a Church

1. If you had to resign from a church what was the reason?

2. Did your resignation come at a time of your choosing? If not, how did you deal with the fallout? How did God help you through that time in your life?

3. How did your family respond? Did you tell them the reason? Were you able to protect them from what you may have experienced?

4. What did the board think when you resigned? The church?

5. What are some reasons you would resign from your church? Does your board know these reasons? Does your wife?

## Using Guilt to Manipulate Church Members

1. Does your church have an unspoken rule that members must attend every service?

2. Do you look at those who do not attend every meeting differently than those who are more regular in their attendance?

3. Do your sermons tend to uplift or condemn your congregation? What would they say?

4. Would people in your church believe from your preaching that God is more pleased with those who are more obedient to Him than those who are less obedient?

5. Do you believe God's blessing on your ministry is the result of your obedience?

# The Reformed Church

I did not like being in the position of looking for a new church. No one likes being an outsider, the new person who has to answer questions from those who are already part of the group. If you are the new person, you know nothing about the history of the church: you don't know how the church is organized, you don't know the dynamics of the church (who is really in charge, who the main families are, who might be mad at whom and for what reason), you are going in blind. It usually takes a few weeks or months to discover if you will fit into the church; if not, you have to begin the search again. People want different things out of church, have different expectations, and need some time to look a church over and find out if it will work for them in terms of philosophy, kids' ministry if you have kids, the preaching, the doctrine, the music, etc. It takes time to sort all of this out. There are two errors that people make in choosing a new church.

The first is that people do not take the time to figure these things out, and they make a decision too quickly. They may not realize that they have expectations of what they want from church, and if they are aware of these expectations and have not talked about them as a family, if they are not met when they join the church, dissatisfaction can set it, even if it is subconscious. The other problem is that people do have a list of expectations that they want from a church, and they can never find one that meets those expectations. Whatever the reason, they attend one church until it falls short in some respect, then they go to another church for a time, and the process is repeated until eventually this type of person just stops going to church because no church ever works for them.

I did not want to be that person. I knew that no church was going to be perfect, but I did have some basic expectations, especially regarding the leadership. I had been a Christian for about thirteen years and had sat under four pastors, three of whom had come up short (Edmund, Matthew, and Jeffrey) and one who was a wonderful, decent man who had a different philosophy of ministry that left me with nothing to do in the church (I did not count Marvin or the pastor before Jeffrey; they were not around long enough to have a real impact on my life).

My wife and I again took stock of our situation and found that there was a Reformed church in the city that was doctrinally conservative, so we decided to give it a go. We were not really strict Calvinists (we did not believe in infant baptism, for example), but it was a Reformed/Calvinistic church, and that appealed to me. My wife would have gone to any church that taught the Bible; she was much less interested in the nuances of doctrine, more so in relationships. So we showed up one Sunday morning, little kids in tow, and walked in the door.

Churches deal with new people in a couple of ways. They either greet them and let them look around and get a feel for the place, or they smother them as soon as they step into the lobby. As with most things, the best practice is probably found somewhere between these extremes. You want to acknowledge people as being visitors, see if they want to talk, and if so, it is appropriate to engage them in some basic conversation. "Are you from the neighborhood? How did you hear about us?" Churches underestimate the importance of greeters and first impressions; the old saying that you only get to make one first impression really applies to churches, and churches that have untrained or overzealous greeters can turn off visitors even before they get into the auditorium and have sung the first song. Most visitors want to look around, get a feel for what is going on, and be acknowledged but not overwhelmed. The worst thing you can do is to absolutely ignore visitors. I have heard stories from my friends who visited churches and were left standing by themselves both before and after the service, and no one likes feeling isolated in a large group.

We came about fifteen minutes before the service was going to start because we had to find out what to do with our kids. Can I be honest and say that while churches are always looking for new members, most churches covet young families? Young families bring instant growth; our family would represent a 3 percent increase in this church if we stayed. Families with children tend to be a little more stable in their church attendance and longevity as well; studies show they are not as likely to leave once they have become members. Plus the parents are more likely to become involved in some type of ministry because they usually want their kids to go to the youth functions, programs, and events. So when a new family shows up as visitors to a church, you can expect that the church will make an effort to bring them into the fold. This church did just that, and on that first service, I am not exaggerating that at least half the congregation greeted us and told us different things about the church, its programs (especially for kids), its history, and its doctrine (I was specifically asked if I was looking for a Reformed church).

Though they were way too eager to communicate with us, I did not look on this as a bad thing, though it was kind of overwhelming. The church had been in existence for about sixty years, and had a good generational mix. It would turn out that there were four main families in the church; they had been there since the church was founded, with now three generations represented in the membership. The middle generation was about our age and had kids the same age as ours, so there was the possibility of connecting with people in our stage of life. The service was pretty similar in form to what we were used to but had a few Presbyterian touches. They said the Apostles Creed nearly every week in unison, they recited the Lord's Prayer together on a regular basis, and nearly all of the men wore suits and ties. I did not own a suit, but I did have a few ties, so the next week I wore one. I just wanted to blend in so I did not think anything about it. The formality of the service was balanced by the friendliness of the people, who went out of their way to incorporate us into the church.

There weren't any other newcomers to the church during the time we began attending, so we sort of stood out from everyone else.

This church had something that the other churches we had gone to did not: small groups that met in homes during the week. After a time, we joined one of these groups; this helped us feel more at home, and we developed one relationship with a family that has continued to this day. We did not visit any other churches; this one seemed to fit. We did not see any warning signs that might have given us pause (though we were still pretty young and had much to learn about how churches function and operate behind the scenes). I had a new job as an independent contractor for a local distribution company, delivering their product to homes and businesses. I would have this job for twenty-eight years. It offered me a lot of freedom in regards to my time and energy, and it paid a little more than a living wage. New job, new church, and new baby (our last child would be born during our time at this church): things were pretty good for us. We look back at that time as the *Little House on the Prairie* years, though in thinking about it, the Ingalls were always having some kind of crisis in their lives, which would also be true of us, though we could not conceive of something really bad happening to us in the future. Like I said, we were pretty naive and innocent.

The pastor of the church was about fifteen years older than I was and had four kids, two of whom were teenagers. His wife, though a college graduate, cleaned houses to make extra income for the family. I guess she did not want to work full time and wanted the flexibility she had doing that type of work. She did not play the piano, was very quiet, and seemed a little world-weary; I seldom saw her smile or laugh. I guess being the mother of teenagers and a pastor's wife brought a lot of challenges into her life, and it showed in her demeanor and personality. The pastor, whose name was Derrick, was very warm, funny, and did not seem to exhibit any of the stresses that Matthew or Jeffrey or even Edmund had shown. Which is another way of saying that he was pretty comfortable with who he was and what he was doing with his life. He would serve at the church for almost fifteen years and then go on the mission field to end his career. He and his wife had served in the Peace Corps before going into the ministry, and I think this gave him a balance to life that served him pretty well. He and I got along well, he was open to talking about the books I was reading, and gave me the opportunity to teach an adult class when the teacher went on vacation.

It seemed that I would be able to find a ministry at this church for which I was grateful. The denomination that the church belonged to was a traditional Reformed denomination, which had split off from another denomination in the late 1930s because of that denomination's tendency toward liberalism. The new denomination founded a seminary, which would become one of the most influential Reformed seminaries in the country. So the historical context of this church was one of standing for the truth against those whom they did not consider to be orthodox (does this sound familiar?). Their focus was on keeping the new denomination true to the historic creeds of Christianity, especially in the Reformed tradition represented by Calvinism. I agreed with all of that, but I did not as yet see that many Reformed churches feel that they were standing against the tide, so to speak, and their focus was to teach and preach correct doctrine. This unfortunately causes most churches in that tradition to be inwardly focused, with the result that they have no outreach or engagement with those who are lost, unless they happen to walk in the front door.

Reformed churches also tend to be very highly structured, with lots of committees; some have presbyteries (groups of churches in a geographical area that meet together frequently) and assemblies (where representatives from all of the churches meet once a year to make sure they are all still doctrinally pure. To run this type of organization takes a lot of the pastor's time and energy and means that the average member invests a lot of time in just being at the church. This isn't necessarily bad; it is just a reality, but it can reduce the focus of your Christian experience to what happens at church, leaving little time for life in the "real world" because you are always going to church for some reason.

Churches that have lots of structure and meetings develop the tendency to judge people by how many meetings they attend. The more meetings and involvement you have in church, the better you are viewed. Leaders are constantly asking the question, "Have you seen _________________? I haven't seen them for two weeks. Does anyone know what is going on?" Leaders get nervous when members do not attend all of the church's services, meetings, or programs. They can think those members are less committed to the church and may be (heaven forbid) considering leaving the church. So some churches consciously or unconsciously tend to have lots of meetings to anchor people to the church, though sometimes this has the opposite effect and either drives people away or burns them out.

As a family we went to church twice on Sunday and had a small group during the week. There were other events during the year that occupied us, and we spent time with one particular family at the church whom we were close to. We were pretty happy with the church for a number of years, but this family we were close to chose to leave because the church was too inwardly focused for them. They moved to a church in the suburbs that was relatively new and had a much more contemporary focus. This was really difficult for us, but we did not let the relationship go. We continued to see them on a regular basis.

The church that they chose to attend would grow to become what would be called a mega church, a new phenomenon that was just coming to be recognized in the evangelical world. Because they had attended the old church for many years, their loss was keenly felt, but they were pretty insistent with the leaders that they needed to move the church into the twentieth century and find a way to become outwardly instead of inwardly focused. They left on good terms, did not cause any hard feelings, and continued to socialize with some of the families in the church for years to come. Their leaving was on a philosophical basis, which they were able to clearly articulate to the pastor and elders, though they were just "laymen" and had no formal training. They were not as committed to the Reformed faith as many in the church, so the anchor that held many to the church did not apply to them. I think they basically just wanted to see people come to Christ in whatever church they attended, and they knew that was not going to happen there.

It was at about that time that I got an opportunity to teach on a regular basis. They had various elective classes for the adults before the worship service and offered me the chance to teach whatever I wanted for a quarter. I decided to teach on Romans 5-8, emphasizing the new identity and nature of the Christian. I had a professor at the Bible college who had greatly influenced me by his teaching on this subject. His main thought was that though all men are sinners and in need of the salvation that Christ offers, when people accept that gift, they are made children of God and their nature is changed from a sinner to a saint, and consequently they have worth, status, and identity as God's children that they did not have before. The practical application of this truth is that believers do not need to continue to look upon themselves as miserable sinners but can rejoice that they are someone loved and cherished by the God of the universe. This may not sound too earth shaking to you, but this truth can be easily misunderstood. No one who has read the Bible with an open mind will deny that it teaches that man is a sinner, alienated from God. The problem is, many Christians still have that view of themselves after they have become saved. They know they are going to heaven, know they are God's children, but still feel unworthy before God, still just a miserable sinner saved by grace. If you teach this truth (on the new identity a believer has in Christ), you have to do it with tact and wisdom, bringing people along slowly; otherwise, they will hear you saying that once you become a Christian you no longer sin or that you are denying the sinfulness of man. I knew all of this and was careful how I presented this truth, which, as it would turn out, was new to everyone in the class.

It was also at this time we had been attending for five years, and I was asked if I would consider becoming an elder. This was a big thing in the Reformed Church; elders are all equal in position and authority, and some Reformed churches even ordain their elders. There is a process to becoming an elder in that denomination. You have to study the Westminster Confession of Faith (a document that dates from the 1600s written by theologians in England that has served as a doctrinal statement for a number of Reformed denominations), and be examined as to your life and ministry and what you believe. I was already along in this process when I began teaching the class, but the process would be stopped in its tracks, and I never became an elder.

What happened was this: the man who had been having the most difficulty in my class with what I was teaching went to the elder board and said basically that I was teaching heresy and asked what they were going to do about it. I did not know any of this until later, but by then it was too late. The pastor had known me for five years, we had talked for hours about the Bible and theology, he knew the books I was reading, and he must have known that I was no heretic.

The irony was that the man who had accused me had been at the church less time than I had and was—how shall I say this—kind of crazy. He was about my age, had five kids, and I hardly ever heard his wife speak during the whole time they attended the church. He and his wife were into the whole natural way of living. Everything had to be organic, and at church dinners they would bring their own food so that their kids did not by accident ingest any sugar or chemicals. This type of living separates you from nearly everyone else on the planet, and if you are not careful, you can develop a superior attitude that only you are doing what is right for your family and everyone else is wrong in how they live.

You can see how this attitude might transfer itself into the world of theology and doctrine; you look with suspicion on anyone who does not speak, sound, or act like you do. The right thing for the pastor and the leadership to do would have been to just come and talk with me. But no elder or the pastor came to talk with me, so I did not know that behind the scenes the process of making me an elder was put on hold.

What they did was to send an elder to my class to see what I was teaching. This elder just showed up one Sunday morning (we had been going for a number of weeks by then) and listened to my lesson. He asked a few questions, came back the next week, and then was gone. (In contrast to the man who had a problem with my teaching, this man, during a conversation I had with him on a men's retreat, could not remember the last time he had eaten a piece of fruit. He was big on meat and potatoes.) I found this a little strange but thought nothing of it. I was supposed to meet with the elders that week to complete the elder process but was told that the meeting would be on hold for the time being. When I asked why, I was told there was some question about my doctrinal fitness. The man who told me this could have phrased it differently, and I would not have been quite as shell-shocked as I was. My doctrinal fitness? What on earth were they talking about?

Then he explained what had happened—the man with the questions, the elder coming to the class, how they had to stop everything while they investigated what the man had said. I politely asked him why they needed to investigate anything; all they had to do was come and talk to me. That was not how they did things, he explained. I would have to meet with the elders and explain what I had been teaching. When I explained this to my wife, she was aghast. She could not believe that a crazy man who did not understand what I was teaching could derail the whole process of me becoming an elder; they had known us longer than the man who had made the accusation. Why believe him over me? Or why not just come and talk to me? Why send in an elder undercover to see if I was teaching heresy? Their response to this would be that they so valued the truth that they took seriously any type of accusation against someone who might be teaching something that was not biblical.

I understand about valuing the truth, but there must be some kind of balance between standing for the truth and preserving some type of unity in the body of Christ. I have come to believe it is unrealistic and probably not in the best interests of any church to have complete agreement on every single variation of biblical truth that is out there among those who attend. What I was offering in my class was a new way to think about what Christ had accomplished for the Christian; indeed, there were numerous Reformed commentators who shared this view about the new nature and position of the believer, that it was wrong to continue to think of yourself in terms of identity and nature as a rebellious, alienated, miserable sinner. Christ's work and God the Father's adoption of us as His children have not only changed our basic natures from sinner to saint but have brought us into a new familial relationship with God that is not consistent with viewing ourselves as sinners (Neil Andersen is probably the best current writer of these themes).

The man who had gone to the elders was questioning whether I believed in the sinfulness of man and in complete sanctification (that it was possible to cease from sinning). No one else in the class came to these conclusions, but because one person felt I was straying into possible heresy, the elders had to get involved. Churches form denominations to keep their doctrinal distinctives intact; many people choose a church because it fits what they believe about the Bible; most people just accept what the church teaches without really exploring for themselves if it is what the Bible teaches or not. Traditional Reformed churches are prone to having really fine lines on what they believe; they do not allow their elders to deviate from their confessional documents and will on occasion have actual heresy trials of professors who have written what is considered by the denominational leaders to be inconsistent with the historic Reformed faith.

So that puts what I was going through in a bit of context. This was not a big deal to the elders—it was what their church and denomination did on occasions like this—but it was a big deal to me. There was not anything personal in the actions of the elders, but then none of them had ever been accused of having faulty doctrine, so they did not know how I was feeling. Their clumsy attempt to uncover the truth, their refusal to just come and talk to me without making it a formal "investigation," their inability to realize that the man who was making the charge was not in any way really qualified to know what he was talking about, all of these facts put the elders in a really bad light to my wife and me. We liked these men but were seeing how a commitment to Reformed theology and a particular form of church government could take normal people and turn them into a tribunal that acted without much common sense and without thinking about how their actions might be interpreted by the one being investigated.

I met with them one evening, and let me tell you they were very sheepish. They did not want to be there, and I think knew they had gone about this in a clumsy, ham-handed kind of way. I was ready to go over the passages in question (Romans 6-8) and felt that I could easily prove that what I had taught was found in the Bible and was not in any was heretical. Well, we never got around to looking at the Bible. The chairman of the elders wanted us to look into the Westminster Confession of Faith as the standard by which we would determine what was right and wrong. When I asked why we didn't just look at the Bible, he said that was not how they dealt with issues like this. I had read some parts of the Confession but was not familiar with it and asked them why we would use the opinions of other men to determine what we believed. It came down to this: they were more comfortable with the Confession of Faith than the Bible.

That was it for me. I told them that I could not participate in a discussion of what was right and wrong biblically without using the Bible, and I excused myself and went home. They were not expecting this and just let me go without comment. I don't know what would have happened if I had submitted to the whole process. My guess is that we might have worked everything out; they would have eventually discovered that there wasn't anything heretical going on in my little class. This was now the second time that I had expressed an opinion in a church and had been set upon by the leadership. As a young man, these actions tore at my self-confidence, and I asked myself what I had done wrong to make these people think I was a bad person. Because I was young and did not have much experience in life (though it seemed like I was getting an education in bad church leadership), I did not have a context to put these actions in. Had I a little more maturity, I would have realized that there wasn't anything personal in this; it was just the way they dealt with things like this in their church. Because they did not have that many incidences like this, I believe this contributed to the awkwardness of how they handled the situation.

As I mentioned earlier, people get their feelings hurt in churches all the time. Sometimes it is completely innocent—someone says something to someone else that hits a nerve that the person who said the words was unaware of. Sometimes the pastor will say something in a message that brings offense to a person in the congregation, and hurt feelings result. A new program or change in the structure of a church can bring hurt feelings if it changes the role or responsibility of those who were invested in the old program or structure and were not brought in on the change process. Lack of clear communication between leadership and the congregation over issues or programs or philosophy can cause problems in a church. The scenarios in a church that can cause hurt and pain and confusion are endless. The problem is not the hurt feelings, which are probably inevitable in any group as diverse as a church; the problem is resolving these situations once you know about them and restoring and repairing those relationships.

This type of ministry requires a lot of wisdom, patience, grace, and the ability to ask for and receive forgiveness if necessary. If someone had come to me and said, "We really blew this. We handled the situation badly. What can we do to solve this situation?" then we might have been open to staying, but that never happened. I could have just sucked it up and let it all play out, but again I was not mature enough to do that, and there is no doubt that my own pride entered into the equation as well. I had been accused of something that was not true, had not really been given a chance to defend myself, so see you later. I did not immediately leave, but the die was cast. Because our best friends had left earlier and moved to another church, it made the move easier. Plus, we had moved to the suburbs about a year earlier and were now much closer to the church our friends attended than to the Reformed church.

## Principles for the Pastor

1. *How to assimilate new people.* For most pastors, it is not enough that they get a continual stream of new visitors; most would like to see some of them become part of the church. There are no reliable statistics that I know of that indicate what percentage of visitors become members; my guess is that churches have too many variables to come up with numbers that work for even your average evangelical church. I once had an elder tell me that you ought to keep at least one out of every ten visitors. Based on what?

   I believe there are some principles that can help assimilate those who have shown an interest in the church by visiting more than a few times. After someone visits our church more than twice, we feel it is appropriate to ask them to lunch. Having lunch after church is pretty informal and nonthreatening, there is a set time limit, you are in a neutral location (as opposed to your home or theirs), and everyone has to eat. Some churches might have a visitor's class or a pastor's reception that newer folks might be comfortable with. Always phrase an invitation in such a way so people have the luxury to say no; let them get used to the church at their own pace. If they are interested, they will join in their own time. Pastors and members can scare people away by being overeager (this is especially true of those who are not Christians; everything is new to them). If a church is trying to assimilate those who are already Christians, they would probably be open to a pastoral visit, but again, give them the luxury to say no without making them feel any guilt.

2. *What to do about small groups?* Nearly every church now has some form of small groups. In the last generation, it has been

realized that a congregation needs some type of structure where people can do life together. The biggest challenge of the pastor will be training those who lead these groups; you cannot just put people into a Bible study group and expect them to relate, grow, and learn together. There is no lack of material to use in these types of settings, but there is a lack of material on how to train small group leaders.

Small groups have life cycles just like churches; most work best with a set time limit, usually one to three years. If these groups are centered on discipleship as opposed to evangelism, consider having them segregated into men's and women's groups. If husbands and wives are together, they will not share things that they would in a group composed of their own sex. Once groups have started, keep them closed. If you have outreach groups, they can continually add new members, but those in a discipleship group need a closed group to develop trust, intimacy, and some measure of accountability. My suggestion is that the pastor attend a group but not lead a group, unless there are no other qualified leaders (if there are no qualified leaders, the pastor's first job is to train some). If the pastor does attend a group, it can be a good place to learn how to become a good listener. Because the pastor is usually the center of every church function, it will be good to have a place where he can be a participant and not the leader.

3. *The pastor's wife.* If a pastor thinks his job is difficult, know that his wife lives with expectations on her that can be even more demanding than the ones that constantly fill her husband's life. The role of the pastor's wife has changed over the years. In the previous generation, it was usually expected that his wife would be an unpaid staff member, know how to play the piano, be seen and not heard, and have a smile pasted on her face at all times to indicate her heavenly disposition. Most pastors' wives who have been surveyed by various organizations (Focus on the Family, The Barna Group),

say she is not happy that her husband is a pastor. She feels everything her husband does about his church experience, mostly because she can read his moods and sense what he is feeling.

If a man is going to be in the ministry for any length of time, he has got to figure out how to protect his wife from the difficulties associated with being a pastor. A pastor must have times that he is not available to the congregation; these times should coincide with his wife's and/or family's schedule. He may have to put his foot down on this. If he doesn't, his life will not be his own, and his wife will come to see the church as a bigger priority than her and the family. I know that most pastors technically have a day or two off, but that seldom stops church or board members from contacting them about things that are usually not in any sense emergencies. Also, if a pastor is working more than fifty hours a week, they are robbing their family of time they need with him. If this is a problem for the board, they are looking at the pastor as their slave. Most pastors' wives (if they don't have small children) have employment outside of the church. My belief is that if your family can manage with mom working, it will help broaden her horizons, and as a result she will not become so wrapped up in the workings of the church.

How to protect her from those well-meaning but clueless people in the church who want to corner her in the lobby after the service? I honestly don't know; some situations defy easy answers. I do know that one thing a man can do to help her survive being a pastor's wife is to not bring his work home with him. If a pastor has to talk about his work, he should find another pastor to meet with for lunch once a week. Finally, use a cell phone as the contact phone so that the wife doesn't have to deal with those who call looking for the husband.

# Questions to Ponder

## Assimilating New People

1. How do people in your church generally become members? Would you describe the process as easy or complicated?

2. What is your involvement in bringing new people into the church as members?

3. How often do you take visitors out to lunch after the service? Do you think this is appropriate?

4. How do you determine what visitors you will call on? Does your board have an expectation of you in this matter?

## Small Groups

1. What percentage of your adult members are involved in small groups? What percentage do you think is realistic?

2. Do you think small groups should meet in homes or at the church? Is one location better than another?

3. How do you choose your material?

4. How do you monitor your small groups?

5. How do you know if they are being effective and fulfilling the purpose you have for them?

6. Have you been in a small group as a participant?

## The Pastor's Wife

1. If your wife had her way, would you be in the ministry?

2.  Is your wife expected to do ministry in the church, or is this her decision to make? What does the church expect? What does the board expect? What do you expect?

3.  What do you do to find time to be with your wife in a setting where church is not mentioned?

4.  Do you have times when your church knows you are not available?

5.  Does your wife have realistic expectations of how difficult your position is?

6.  On a scale of 1 to 10, how content is your wife with her role as the "pastor's wife"?

7.  What can you do to make her life less tense and stressful, and help her have a better church experience?

# The Mega Church

I don't know what expectations we had for the new church. It had been founded about seven years previously and had grown to about two thousand people by the time we began to attend. Compared to the Reformed Church, this church had no traditions, was not associated with any denomination, and had a much more contemporary style of worship. It also had three co-pastors; the three men who founded the church shared the pulpit, which was unusual at that time. They had a network of small groups and a pastor to oversee them, which was also different. It felt kind of strange to attend a church that was viewed as "trendy" (they were one of the first evangelical churches in the area to not have a Sunday evening service, a pattern that nearly all other churches would follow in the next few years). Most of the people who attended had come from more traditional churches; that was one of the reasons that the church grew so fast, though there were new converts as well. It was good to attend a church where we had really good friends who made the adjustment a little easier. The reality was that I was never going to be able to teach a class (due to space limitations they only had two Sunday school adult classes and had seminary professors in those positions) or perhaps have any type of ministry; maybe I could lead a small group in the future, but that was about it.

One of the reasons we chose this church was that it had a large youth group that we hoped would become a home for our kids, who were getting close to being teenagers. Though we tried, we could never get our kids integrated into the youth group, which was a real disappointment to us as parents. Overall, we enjoyed the experience of being in a new type of church, one that would become a model for other churches in the years to come.

None of the three men who led the church had ever been the pastor of a church before, so everything that they did was for the first time. Because the church grew so rapidly, it felt like they were constantly catching up to the numbers of people who were attending. They kept adding services until there were three on Sunday morning. They had traffic directors, and they even had people to direct traffic into the auditorium. The layout of the building had not been designed for the amount of people that were now attending. You had to maneuver your way around groups of people who were standing in the lobby either before or after a service and hurry to find a seat. They did not have a worship team, but rather they had different people responsible for different services. They gave these people the freedom to choose the music, the order of the service, everything up to the message. Every week the atmosphere of the service was different as people brought their own unique style to the service. Some weeks there would be just one person playing the piano leading everyone, the next week there would be perhaps six people on stage with different instruments, and the next week something completely different. This style of worship was completely unique to this church and was probably one of the reasons that the church grew so fast. Most evangelical churches used the same people with the same instruments resulting in the same style of worship every week, so this style of worship was fresh and new.

Try changing the format of your Sunday morning service and sees what happens. What will happen is that some people will have a coronary, something that can definitely add drama to a Sunday morning. At this church *different* was the established norm, so no one cared if the worship format varied every week.

Why did this church grow so fast? The church began as a split from another church where two of the pastors were serving, one as associate pastor and one as youth pastor (the other founding pastor was a friend from seminary). They took about half the church with them and were off and running. Ten years later they had at least two thousand people attending (they did not have formal members, another departure from how most churches functioned) and were still growing. They did not have a strategy for this growth; it just happened. I think that because everything they did was different from how other churches operated, this created a buzz in the metropolitan area about the church that no other ministry had at the time. For example, they did not take an offering during the service. They had a few boxes located near the doors to the auditorium that people could use; they mentioned this once in a while in the service. I have already talked about how the music was different from other churches in the area (though the style would be copied by other churches). The teaching was different in that you had at least three men who shared that responsibility (later they would add other men to the rotation), which meant that people did not specifically come to the church to hear one person teach.

There was another reason that played into the rapid growth of the church—it was located in a growing area on the outskirts of the metro area, with new homes and subdivisions going up in the general area of the church. In church growth strategy, there is a phrase known as "sewer growth" or "sewer theology." It means that churches tend to grow where there are new sewers being put in because new homes are being built, resulting in growing population base. People who are just moving into a new home may also be looking for a new church.

Not every church that is started in a suburb succeeds to the extent that this church did, but the location of the church did undoubtedly help its growth. Physically, it was located just off the main highway so that it could be seen by everyone driving into or out of the city from the south. With all of these factors in place, it was almost preordained that the church would grow, which it did. Church planters have tried to duplicate the success of churches that have shown steady growth in terms of location, music, building, teaching, small groups, and other factors, but if it was that easy, there would be churches like this one on every corner of the suburbs. There are undoubtedly some principles that can be transferred, but I think some churches succeed and some fail for reasons that cannot be duplicated or even explained. If you asked the men involved in this church why it grew so fast, they would give you different answers, answers that might even be contradictory. Then there is, of course, the plan and blessing of God involved in the process, which will be experienced differently by each church. I even think that those involved in the leadership of that church might think that the growth of the church was too fast, and that left them scrambling to keep up the demands of the ministry in terms of space, programs, staff, strategy, and future planning (a problem that many pastors would love to have).

When we arrived, it was obvious that they would need to construct some buildings to accommodate the various ministries they wanted to pursue, as well as the growth of the school (which our oldest daughter attended). The church had bought several temporary buildings to use as they pursued options for growth. The property they had was maxed out. The land next to them on each side was farmland, and neither party was interested in selling any part of their land to the church. One neighbor in particular was not happy with the church because of all the traffic that used the road; what used to be a sleepy little country lane (it was a two-lane road) was now completely congested from 8:00 a.m. to 1:00 p.m. on Sundays and had a lot of traffic during the week due to the school and other activities that happened at the church. I don't imagine that person ever thought that a church would go up next to his home, particularly a church that would mushroom into a mega church within a few years. The leadership had a plan to build a new auditorium and office buildings on the current site. With all of the growth, they had to do something. I don't think that it occurred to them to start another church; that would have been an option that could have resulted in even greater growth and created opportunity for more ministry and new momentum even as that church had done years previously.

The mega church continued to grow, and the facilities were getting pretty maxed out. If something was not done in terms of adding space, the church faced the possibility of not having enough room for everyone who wanted to attend. They could not realistically add another service, nor could they offer any type of Christian education for most of the people who attended due to a lack of available rooms. The leadership decided to build some new structures on the property, including a new worship center, a program that would cost a huge amount of money. The church planned a service to gather everyone together and go over the plans, celebrate the church's growth, and then ask for pledges to raise the money to be able to proceed.

The church at that time did not want to take on any significant debt for this project and wanted to get the congregation to pledge most of the money needed. I was not able to attend this meeting because we had little kids and did not really have a babysitter at this point in our life (it wasn't until our tenth year of marriage that my wife and I went away for a weekend without the kids, a weekend where I got terribly sick). The senior pastor led the meeting and went over the plans; there was a time of worship, pledge cards were handed out to everyone, the cards were filled out and collected, and then everyone went home. This happened on a Saturday night. You can imagine the leadership sitting in a back room at the church where they met (they met in another church that had enough seating to fit most of the congregation) and counting the pledge cards to see if they could proceed with their building plans. They had gone to a lot of effort to set up this meeting, show how the new structures would continue the growth of the church, and solve the existing space problems. What happened was that the total on the pledge cards came up short of what was needed, and not just a little short but a lot short, so much so that there was no way that they could proceed with their plans to enlarge the church facilities.

Churches proceed into dangerous territory when they consider entering into some type of building program. This type of program falls squarely on the shoulders of the pastor. He has to be able to provide the vision for what is needed, rally the church around the project, find a team to oversee the project, and most importantly, find a way to fund the project. There are different ways to accomplish the funding part. Churches can get loans from banks or other lending institutions or they can raise either part or all of the money from the membership. Some churches will not go into debt for any reason; some churches see no problem in getting a loan. Each church has to decide for itself how it will fund this type of project. Depending on the size of the project, it can take months or years to complete the process, and keeping a church together during a building project requires wisdom, grace, and constant communication with the church.

Building projects can overtake a church and become the focal point until they are completed. A wise pastor knows how to keep the church from becoming distracted from its mission by a building project, and many churches have split because of disagreements that have erupted over this type of project. The more planning, communication, and agreement there are at the beginning among the leadership and the congregation, the more chance for success a building project will have. When things go wrong (no building project ever goes completely according to plan), the goodwill created at the beginning of the process will help when expectations have to be lowered concerning either the timing of the project or other problems that will surface.

I expect that the senior pastor at the church had thought that he would have the required pledges to begin the building project, but it was not to be. Those who attended the meeting did not pony up the amount necessary to start the project, so that was that. What should he and the leadership have done at this point? There were a number of options: perhaps realize they had not communicated the need of new buildings well enough to the congregation, perhaps realize that the congregation did not mind things being cramped and crowded, maybe realize that the congregation just did not want to part with any more of their money, perhaps realize that the congregation was not as mature as they thought, or perhaps realize that the congregation may have felt they were being manipulated into doing something they might have done if they had been approached differently. Or the leadership could have sought the Lord and humbly asked from Him a reason why they were turned down by the people they were leading. There were other options to dealing with the crowding. The option of starting another church at this point could have been brought forward, but it was not.

The next day in the morning service, the senior pastor stood before the congregation and announced to them that he was disappointed in them and told us that we were immature and unsupportive of him. I had never heard a pastor in a service tell his flock that they were immature and had made a mistake in not supporting the building proposal. This was different from Matthew bringing this staff down and telling us that we had to follow him as pastor. There were no visitors present, and it was not done in a time set apart to worship God. He seemed very petulant to me, and I wondered what other people were thinking. It would be years before the church built a new worship center. By then our family would be long gone.

After attending for a time, we decided to join a small group. If you desire to grow as a disciple of Jesus, you need to develop relationships with people in your church who will help you with that process. It is just not possible to attend the Sunday morning service and become a mature follower of Christ. The worship service is anonymous, and while it is important for Christians to worship together and learn together corporately, there is no chance to develop habits, character, or virtues that are part of the Christian life. It was not until the 1970s that churches began to develop groups that were more than just another opportunity to learn more about the Bible, groups that would not only learn as a group but pray with each other and share together the circumstances and difficulties of their lives.

Our group was mainly composed of couples. We knew some of them, and others were new to us. My wife and I stayed in the background for almost the entire year. We were polite, joined in the discussion occasionally, attended all of the meetings, but based on some of our past experiences were just a little cautious. The church had called a new assistant pastor, and he was in our group. This man had been the pastor of a large church in the city about twenty years previously, a church that was known for (I kid you not) the pastor not wearing a suit and tie during the Sunday evening service. The senior pastor had sat under this man for a time and had offered him a chance to come on staff as pastor to adults (think of lots of visitation to older people and those in the hospital) when he was out of a job. He was very likable, did not overwhelm the group by talking too much, and fit in nicely with the rest of us. When group ended just before summer, we felt that it had been a good experience and we would join another group in the fall.

During those years at the church, our oldest daughter attended the junior high school that the church had began several years earlier. We had enrolled her when she began to develop signs of rebellion, hoping that by being exposed to Christian teachers and curriculum she might change the course of her life. I know of Christian parents who vehemently oppose this practice, of sending your child to a Christian school because they are disobedient, feeling that rebellious or disobedient children will "infect" those kids that are doing well. We felt that we did not have many options at that point, and we really didn't care what anyone thought about it anyway. Two years at the school did not change the direction of her life in any way, and she did not drag anyone down with her that we knew of, so there was that.

What do you do when a child goes down the proverbial wrong road? We had no experience and no one who was older and wiser who might have gone through something similar who we could talk to and get advice. We had naturally assumed that if you loved your children, taught them about Jesus, and provided them a good role model as loving parents, then they would turn out all right. Here again we were dealing with expectations; our expectations in no way matched our reality, and we were overwhelmed not only with her behavior but with emotions that were all over the place. We had friends with children our age who avoided us because of our daughter. Our younger kids were caught in the wake of our battles with her and did not get the attention they deserved and needed.

During one Sunday morning service, one of the assistant pastors preached a sermon that contained some thoughts that I found pretty silly. It wasn't the interpretation of the Bible that I found bizarre but the application that he took from what he thought the Bible was saying. I respected this man because he had participated in some of our pro-life activities (he did not break any laws but rather stood on the sidewalk as a show of support) and I was puzzled by what he had said. I tried to get up to the front to talk to him after the service just to ask him a question or two but was unable. There were other people talking to him, and there was another service that would begin shortly.

I have no idea why what he said in his message stuck in my brain. I really don't. In the thousands of messages that I have listened to over the years, I can count on one hand the number of times I have ever talked to the teacher or preacher to comment on what he had said. I believe that the person who is teaching should be given the freedom to give the message that God has given him, and unless there is something bordering on heresy, what's the point? In all of my casual discussions with other Christians down through the years, I have yet to have a conversation with someone about a theological or biblical subject where I changed their mind to embrace my opinion or interpretation of whatever it is we were talking about. That does not seem to be the usual way that God brings about change in how we view the Bible. Usually our views change over time; sometimes we might not even be aware that we have changed until we engage someone else in conversation or hear a message and realize that we have a different view than we used to have.

The views that I have changed over the years usually have come about because of books that I have had time to read through and digest. That is a long explanation to say that in looking back I have no idea why I sat down and wrote him some observations on what he had said and how I had a different take on what he had spoken on. Sometimes you do things that will have unintended consequences that you cannot know at the time and would never have done if you had known what would result from your actions. Believe me, I wrote simply and as matter-of-factly as I could (remember that I had some experience with leadership not being open to other opinions) and was not expecting any type of reply. I was not as cynical as I would become later and just hoped that he might see another point of view on the application that he brought out from the text.

One of the things that I have learned in the years since is that if you are going to stand in front of people and tell them, "This is what I believe the Bible is saying," you had better be able to respond to those who might have questions or observations about what you have said. One of the results of the Reformation was to allow people to interpret the Bible individually and not be forced to believe what the church was teaching if it did not square with your interpretation of the Bible. So I mailed the letter and thought that was that.

I believe that God directs the course of our lives and that one of the ways that He does this is by changing our circumstances through events that we might not be aware of at the time. For example, my first year out of high school I attended Biola College (this was before I went to Bible college) and commuted from home the first semester. The second semester I wanted to live on campus and went one day to fill out an application to live in a dorm. There would have been no reason for the school to not allow me to move on campus. They encouraged those who were able to live in dorms if possible. But the person who had the form was not there that day, and because of some other events that happened in my life that week, I decided to live at home the rest of the year. I only went to Biola that one year. In all likelihood, had I lived on campus, I would have continued there the next year (I had a scholarship in speech and debate, which would, in the last two years, have paid most of the tuition and board) and eventually graduated. It also meant that I would not have married my wife. We were not yet a couple at this point. It is more than likely that, being on the campus full time, I would have become involved with someone else. All this to say that that one-page letter would begin a process that would result in our leaving the church and nearly drive my wife to stop going to church altogether.

Within a day or two of mailing the letter, I got a call from a secretary at the church asking me if I could meet with the pastor to whom I had mailed the letter. I said sure, no problem. I drove to the church at the appointed time and waited for a while to see the pastor. He came out and ushered me into his office with a word of greeting, and then we were off. I mean he was off. I was there for about half an hour and said about ten words the whole time. What followed was a *tirade* (I use this word because of the emotion involved) not so much against what I had written but against my having written anything at all. He began by telling me that he had never had anyone write him anything negative before and was taken aback that I would do this (it was interesting to me that he viewed someone else's opinion on a subject as being negative).

Then he went on to tell me about all the people who had told him how good his message was and that I was the only person who had found anything wrong with what he had said (if he meant this to try and make me feel bad, it did not work; I had been down that road before). As he went on and on, I honestly thought that he was a little crazy. I mean, I was a nobody, just a person who sat in the auditorium each week. I had no constituency. I wasn't a leader or elder or teacher or anything. Who was I to merit all of this anger? When I saw that this was not going to be a discussion of what he had said (we never talked about what he had said in his message), I just wanted to leave. The one thing that I was able to say was that I was sorry for writing anything; had I known it was that big a deal, I never would have bothered him. Then he prayed, and that was that. I left the office into the bright sunshine of the afternoon, unutterably sad, knowing that I would never get to do anything in that church. I sat in my car for a moment and then drove home to the chaos that was our home life.

Our daughter had gotten pregnant by this time, and my wife and I were dealing with the reality of having a sixteen-year-old having a baby. Things had gotten so bad earlier in the year that we had sent her to a Christian counseling facility in California for a month; things were that out of control. When she returned, she seemed a little better but got involved with the guy who would be the father of her child (it was against her will, but we did not find out about this until later). We needed help, someone to talk to, and thought of the pastor who had just come on staff who had been in our small group. He was older and had been in the ministry for nearly forty years. Surely he would be able to help us and give us some counsel on how to deal with this situation, though what we really needed was just someone to talk to who would let us get out all of the hurt and pain that we were feeling.

He agreed to meet with us in our home and arrived one evening to talk with us and our daughter. We had told him about the situation and expected him to share some wisdom or something with us that might help us or her in this rather delicate situation. He arrived at the house, and the first thing that caught my eye was that he was wearing sweats that had the logo of the local sports team. I really do not care what people wear, but I did think that this was odd. He began by sharing with us what a great workout he had at the gym and how his day had been going.

You have to picture this: our daughter was sitting on the couch next to my wife eight-months pregnant, the proverbial elephant in the room. We had asked him to come over to help us in this situation, at least to listen, but as the minutes wore on, it was all small talk. And it was all one sided. We hardly said anything. We could have turned the subject to the issue at hand, but he was in charge of the conversation, which he kept firmly focused on himself. I felt like I was having an out-of-body experience, watching the scene unfold but not being a part of anything being said.

There are times in life when you just give up, and this was one of them. I just gave up and realized nothing was going to change. There was no magic wand that this man had that would help us. He really didn't care about what we were going through; nobody really cared, from what I could tell, and what was the point of it all? I missed the last part of his visit; my mind was gone. My wife said a few things, more small talk, but he only stayed about thirty minutes, and then he was gone. We had not talked about how you deal with a pregnant teenager. I don't remember if we prayed together. We did not agree to meet again; it was just over. I didn't want to say anything to my wife until after our daughter had left, and then all I could say was that that was the strangest thing I had ever experienced in my life, and then I went to bed. I was not angry or disappointed. I was not feeling anything and realized that we were on our own; our church would not play any part in helping us get through this difficult time in family.

There was no way that I could go to anyone in leadership and tell them about this experience; no one would have believed me (a few years later this pastor would be dismissed from the church for causing dissension). I would not have believed me either. I suppose I could have followed up with the pastor, but I didn't. We were not quite ready to give up on the church; there were other pastors, so my wife made an appointment with the youth pastor to talk about our other kids, who were having some difficulty breaking into the youth group. Because our youth group had meant so much to us as teenagers, we wanted our kids to become a part of this church's youth group, but they just did not like it. They complained that the kids who attended the school at the church would not associate with them, and they felt out of place. I think there was some truth to this, but the reality was they just did not think of church in the same way that we had when we were their age. So my wife spent some time with the youth pastor, hoping that he might have an idea or take some interest in our kids, but nothing came of this visit. Nothing.

You begin to wonder after a while when you have several negative experiences with leadership at the church you attend what is wrong with you. Had we done something wrong? Was God mad at us? Didn't He care about the situation we were in? Wasn't the church supposed to help people like us in desperate straits? Was the church too big to be able to help everyone, even those who came begging for some kind of help? (Some people would think and continue to think that this was the greatest church in the world; your experience, of course, will not be the same as someone else's.)

We had already left three churches, and those experiences had not been pleasant. We did not want to start over again. How many times can you do that? Who has that much emotional energy to keep trying to find a place that will love and accept you and help you in time of need? My wife was about done with church. She had been hurt about as much as she could take, and if I had said, "That's it. We're done with church," my guess is that she might have said, "That is fine with me." I doubt if we would have quit church entirely, but we might have sat out for a while, which is what we did, though we would continue to attend church in the future.

Years later that church would go through some difficult times. As I mentioned earlier, every church goes through a life cycle, and when this church was about thirty years old, the board and the pastor (the three men who had started the church had evolved into the oldest one becoming the senior pastor) had some real differences of opinion on the future vision of the church. The board asked the pastor to leave, there were confidentiality agreements signed by members of the staff who would also be asked to leave, and there were meetings with the congregation that would go on for hours and hours and leave everyone who attended confused and emotionally exhausted. The church finally had to call in an outside mediation group to help them get through that period. Meanwhile, the church continues to slowly decline, both in numbers and revenue because they have not instituted a plan to re-envision or renew themselves. In some ways, they are a victim of their own success; there have been numerous new churches planted in the area, churches that are siphoning off believers from other churches, just like the mega church did when they started, though that was certainly not their intention.

We knew we had to go to church. We did not know where, but we knew we just could not up and quit. But it did not mean that we had to become involved. We were like a patient being discharged from the hospital; you need time to recover before resuming your normal life and responsibilities. I had not had the opportunity to do anything at the large church; I would not have a ministry for about ten years, all of this in the "prime of my life." We would later refer to this time as being in the wilderness, wandering around without any purpose or direction (at least that we could see at the time).

## Principles for the Pastor

1. *Large churches, the good and the bad.* If pastors are honest with themselves they would probably rather pastor a large church than a small church. In our culture, success is many times defined by bigness. Large churches are looked upon as models to which smaller churches can aspire. Larger churches put on seminars on how to become large; smaller churches do not put on seminars on how to remain small. Pastors of large churches write books and are in demand as speakers in other churches and conferences; pastors of small churches toil in relative anonymity. Since the average church in the US is around one hundred members, most will minister in the world of the small church, with many pastors wishing their church was a mega church and their name was known in the evangelical world.

   What does God think about the size of a church? My guess is that what matters to Him is what happens in the church, not the size of the church. Large churches can do things that small churches cannot. They can spend more money on facilities, they can have higher quality worship (bigger bands, paid worship leader), they will have larger and more dynamic youth ministries, and they will generally have a higher number of people visit than a smaller church. The pastor is probably a dynamite communicator (one reason why the church may be large), and the church will have a large staff to manage the many different ministries of the church.

   That is all good, but there are some realities about large churches that are seldom addressed. Large churches guarantee that those who attend can remain anonymous.

One of my children attended a mega church in a Southern state for two years; no one ever made an attempt to learn her name or anything about her. Large churches have difficulty bringing their members to maturity in Christ. Because large churches are deemed to be successful, most of the focus of the pastor and staff will be centered on refining those things that bring people to the church (music, atmosphere of the service, the pastor's sermon). Most large churches have some type of small group ministry, but the percentage of members who attend varies widely from church to church. Most pastors report that on average only twenty to thirty percent of their congregation attends small groups at least twice a month (see the statistics on pastors at the end of the book).

2. *The challenge of counseling.* One of the responsibilities of a pastor will be to counsel those who come to them with their difficulties, problems, and suffering. Many pastors feel equipped both professionally and personally to counsel people in their times of need; some dread each appointment because it is not one of their strengths, but they do it anyway because it is what people expect. People come to pastors for counsel with different motives. Some have nowhere else to turn, some come because pastors do not charge for their services, and some come because they want something from the pastor other than their words of wisdom. People will tell pastors things in confidence that will disturb them, disgust them, and perhaps alarm them; pastors have to maintain some kind of emotional distance from people's problems if they are going to survive. Many pastors will not enter into long-term counseling relationships. If they cannot help someone after a specific amount of time, they will refer them to a professional.

A word of advice based on dealing with hundreds of pastors over the years: do not counsel women alone, especially in the evening. If you must counsel women, then find a woman in your church who is wise, can keep confidences, and is preferably married to be with you when you deal with a woman who comes for counseling. This usually involves sitting outside your office (your door should have glass in it so you are visible) while you are counseling someone of the opposite sex. If the person desiring counseling finds this awkward or refuses to meet this requirement, send her on to someone else. The evangelical world is filled with pastors who have fallen into sin with those who come to them for counseling. Don't become one of these statistics. (This principle also applies to those of you who have female staff members. I know it is hard, but being alone on a regular basis with female staff members, especially in the evening, is a potential land mine waiting to go off. Be wise, be prudent, and be careful).

3. *Why Christians move from one church to another.* All of us are aware that many Christians move around from one church to another. There are many reasons for this practice, some of which include:

a. **Dissatisfaction with the pastor.** This is perhaps the main reason for Christians moving from one church to another. Since the pastor is usually the face of the church, this is not surprising. If people cannot relate to him, his messages, his personality, or even his family, they will probably leave. If this is the reason why they have left the church, the pastor is going to feel bad, possibly even to the extent of feeling personal rejection. When a man comes to a new church, expect that people will leave. They will compare him to the old pastor. He may not meet whatever expectation they have for a pastor. This also is part of church life. The good thing is that people will join the church who do relate to the new pastor and his ministry, but it may be that they came from a church where the other pastor did not relate to them.

One last caution: those who have left a church because of dissatisfaction with the pastor may have a habit of finding fault with church leadership, so don't be surprised if they find fault with you as well.

b. **New, trendy churches.** Many Christians are drawn to churches that are "the latest thing" and mistakenly think that these churches are better able to meet their needs and expectations regarding church. When the next big thing comes along, they again change churches, etc. etc.

c. **Hurt feelings resulting from conflict with other church members.** People will come to a church from another church where they have had a difficult experience that was not able to be resolved. They bring their hurt, mistrust, and pain to the new church. Sometimes this works out well for everyone involved. In life it is just not possible to resolve every personal issue that will develop between believers (though you should try).

4. *Raising money.* Every pastor will have to raise money. They may not teach a class on this at Bible college or seminary, but the reality is that churches need money to function and more money if they are going to do something out of the normal budget parameters. It is just a fact that the more money churches have, the more ministry they can do. This may seem shallow and "unspiritual," but it is true nevertheless. Because the pastor is the leader and face of the church, this responsibility will fall on him. However a pastor decides to raise money, he should develop a plan with the board or a special committee on how to proceed.

If a pastor is new to this or doing it at his church for the first time, he should go slowly and get all the help he can. The more people he can involve, the better. What happens if he stumbles? What happens if he does not raise the amount he needs? Again, the more people involved, the fewer repercussions will fall on the pastor. If the pastor has a plan, can communicate what the money will accomplish, and what needs it might meet that the church currently has, he will do well. Building projects, though they usually involve the most money, are sometimes the easiest to sell because the need is evident.

5. *How to take criticism.* Few jobs can match the emotional rollercoaster of being a pastor. One moment a pastor is on the top of the world because he has just preached the best sermon of his life and has received compliments from his admiring congregation. The next day he will get a call from a long-time member who tears into him for not visiting their brother-in-law when he was sick, despite the fact that the pastor did not know the man and no one told him he was sick! Realizing that it is inevitable that a pastor will be criticized in his role as pastor will help him deal with it when it happens. If a pastor falls apart emotionally every time someone complains about his ministry or what is happening at the church, he will wreck his family and constantly feel insecure and anxious about his position.

Much of the criticism that pastors will receive from church members will not be personal, but it will still feel that way. Because the pastor is the leader of the church, it is natural that the members will come to him with their complaints about the church. Many people mean well when they come to the pastor with their concerns, complaints, or criticisms; they just do not know how to express them in a manner that is appropriate. As a result, pastors may take something personally that was not meant that way at all. If he can figure out the motives behind the words, this might help when people complain. Because leading the church is his job, and he is the face of the church, it is hard for him not to take criticism personally. People will offer the pastor advice on how to run the church, on why they think this or that will or will not work, how the church used to be so much better under the former pastor, how his wife does not attend every meeting, how he works too much or too little, and my favorite, why the church isn't growing.

One of the best ways to deal with criticism is to realize that those who criticize and complain the most are usually the most unhappy, insecure, and anxious people in the church. If the pastor can find it in his heart to feel compassion on them, it will help in dealing with their words. Many times if people are given the opportunity to voice their complaints to the pastor at a time of his choosing (best to do this somewhere other than the church, perhaps over lunch), this will satisfy them. I think many who are critical just want a chance to be heard; they probably know instinctively the pastor is not going to change the church to what they want. This does not mean the pastor should not address their complaints—he should, in an honest and forthright manner.

If the pastor can assure people that he and the board are acting in unison, it will help take the focus off him. If the complaints and criticisms are coming from a board member, this is more of a challenge. Meeting alone with a board member is an option, but if the criticism is happening in board meetings, it should be dealt with there. Again, the pastor will have to be honest, deal with the issues, and try to keep personality, personal agendas, pride, and emotions in check. Criticism is not always the same as disagreement; it can turn into something more sinister if not dealt with appropriately. Disagreement will usually subside after discussion; criticism can linger because it often involves elements like pride, control, or unresolved personal feelings (bitterness, anger, and unforgiveness). Persons who continually complain and criticize will need to be confronted about their attitude, or it can lead to division in the church and take a toll on the pastor personally.

# Questions to Ponder

## Large Churches

1.  If you are the pastor of a large church, would you say this is specifically the result of your gifts and abilities?

2.  If you are the pastor of a small church, would you say this is specifically the result of your gifts and abilities?

3.  Do you think it matters to God the size of the church you pastor?

4.  Do you think that churches should grow under "normal" circumstances?

5.  Do you think your church will continue to grow or hit a "natural" attendance level?

6.  If you have tried to increase the size of your church and have not been as successful as you thought you would be, how has this affected your confidence? What have been the expectations of your board regarding the size of your church?

7.  Would you rather be the pastor of a smaller or medium-sized church or the associate of a large church?

## Counseling

1.  On a scale of 1 to 10, how gifted do you feel to counsel those who come to you?

2.  How good are you at keeping the confidences of those you counsel?

3.  How long will you generally deal with someone who comes to you for counseling? Weeks? Months? Years?

4. Do you have a professional counselor that you refer people too? Under what circumstances do you refer people to someone else?

5. What is the most common problem that people bring to you?

6. Are you a good listener? Do people feel that they can be open with you? Do they generally want to come back?

7. What successes and failures have you had in terms of counseling? What is your expectation when people come to you for help?

8. Does counseling present temptation to you? In what forms? How do you deal with these temptations?

9. What is your practice in counseling women? Does your wife know what your practice is? Is she okay with it?

10. Are there people in your church who might be gifted in this area of ministry? What would your church think if someone other than the pastor was involved in the counseling ministry?

## Christians Who Move from One Church to Another

1. How do you feel when those who are already Christians join your church? How do you ask them about their prior church experience?

2. What percentage of your new members in a year are already Christians?

3. Does your church care if its growth consists mainly of those who are already Christians?

4. Does your church specifically target Christians who might be looking for a new church by being different from other

churches in terms of music, video, building, programs, style, etc.?

5.  How do you deal with those who come into your church who have just had a bad church experience?

6.  If your church grew by 25 percent in one year and all of the growth came from those who are already Christian, would anyone notice or care?

## Raising Money

1.  What has been your experience in terms of raising money? On a scale of 1 to 10, how difficult is this for you to do?

2.  Does your church have traditional ways to raise money outside of regular giving?

3.  How dependent is your church on members who are rich? How are they approached when the church is trying to raise money, if they are approached at all?

4.  How much time in your board meetings is taken up with issues regarding money? Is this a concern to you?

5.  How supportive has your church been when you have had to go to them for money? How supportive has your board been?

6.  Do you think that if you are able to raise the money you need for your project or need that God approves of the plan? How is God involved in how your church raises money?

## How to Take Criticism

1.  How often do members of your church say things that would be termed critical?

2.  Do these complaints center on any particular area of your ministry?

3.  Do you listen carefully to people's criticism or immediately become defensive?

4.  Do you think that some people are just critical by nature or temperament and thus give less weight to their words?

5.  When do you think criticism becomes sin, or is it always sin?

6.  Generally, do the positive comments you receive balance out the negative? Does this cause you to be on a continual emotional roller coaster, or have you found a way to deal with these ups and downs?

7.  How has God helped you deal with criticism, especially when you feel it is unwarranted?

8.  Do you generally find that older or younger people are most prone to complain to you? What does this say to you, if anything, about those people?

9.  How have you tried to shield your wife from the criticism that you get from church members? Have you been successful?

# The Community Church

We stared going to another church, but I do not remember why we chose it, just like I don't remember a lot of things from that time. It was a smaller church of about two hundred or so, and for the two years that we attended, it was a good fit. We needed to just sit and decompress. We did not ever share with anyone what we had gone through at the other church. I think we just said we desired to go to a smaller church. No one is ever going to question your motives in coming to their church; most of the time they are glad that you are there. I knew one of the pastors from Bible college, so there was some personal connection, but really all we wanted to do was sit. I was not going to say anything, I wasn't going to write anything to anyone, I didn't care if I taught or led a small group, and all that we were able to do was attend. We were not going to put ourselves in the position of being hurt by anyone.

We had no ability at that point to trust anyone. We were dealing with things that we did not or could not share with anyone else. We attended church because it was the right thing to do; we always tried to do the right thing, if not always with the right motivation. If you are going to attend a local church, you should become involved in some way, use the gifts that God has given you, and find ways to minister to others. All we could do at the beginning was show up for worship on Sunday and then go home. We probably seemed somewhat aloof at first; we did not really want to get to know anyone for a while, and we did not want to join a group or become involved in any way.

There are millions of Christians who just attend church and never become involved in a significant manner. They show up for the worship service, and that is pretty much it. They have little personal contact with the church during the rest of the week and are content to express their Christianity in this kind of manner. Most churches measure their success by the number of people who attend the morning service; if that number is growing, or at a number that the leadership has determined to be sufficient, then there is usually a measure of satisfaction. If that number is declining, then there are apt to be discussions among the leadership about how to increase that attendance.

One of the reasons churches measure success by looking at the attendance of the morning service is that it is the only time the whole church is gathered together in one place and can see each other. Churches that routinely fill their auditoriums will be concerned about issues of space, not issues of discipleship. Churches that are not filling their auditoriums will be concerned about how to fill those empty seats—that will become their main priority. I have sat with pastors who have said that they cannot minister or disciple people until they are in the seats. But when those seats become filled, somehow the need to disciple and mature those people isn't the priority that the leadership had said it would be.

The best measure for indicating if a church is serious about discipleship is to count how many of its members consistently are involved in some type of small group. A healthy church will have at least 60-75 percent of its members in a small group where they can learn, pray, relate, be held accountable for their spiritual growth, and care for each other. As I have mentioned before, no one ever became a mature Christian by just going to the Sunday morning worship service. Most pastors and leaders recognize this, and to their credit, most evangelical churches have some sort of small group ministry, but the percentage of members who attend varies considerably from one church to another. Not only are small groups essential to help Christians move ahead in their spiritual journeys, but these groups need trained leaders who know how to move people along in that journey, helping those in their groups to develop habits, character, and virtue. I have sat in many groups where all we did was fill out the answers in some sort of material and discuss the answers together as a group. When we did pray, it was usually centered on those among us (or our friends or family) who were ill. The group was considered a success if it stayed together for a year or managed to get through whatever material was being used, and there was seldom any way to measure if those in the group had moved ahead in their Christian faith.

Though the small group movement has brought added life and relationship building back to the church, it is too often centered on the accumulation of knowledge, of learning more about the Bible. Small groups that are content centered, where most of the time is spent on discussing the lesson, perpetuate the idea that spiritual life is about learning more about the Bible, an idea that has held the church in its grasp for far too long. This idea is the product of the seminary and Bible college system and the fact that Americans seem to value education above all else. Why else would we think that only someone who has graduated from a seminary or Bible college is qualified to be a pastor? Why else would the church turn to "professional" organizations to train those who will lead the church instead of doing the training themselves? This attitude works its way into most everything the church does. The more information we can give to our members about the Bible, the more they will grow. Knowing the Bible is certainly one part of spiritual growth, but knowing that Bible outside of the context of relationship building may only produce Pharisees.

One of the consequences of the priority of teaching biblical content is that many churches become inwardly focused and lose their passion for reaching people with the gospel. When I ask people what the mission or purpose of the church is, many will say it is to worship God, some will say it is to preach the Word, and some will say it is to make disciples (echoing Jesus's words of the Great Commission in Matthew 28:18-20). While all of these are true, it occurred to me many years ago that we will worship God when we get to heaven, we will learn more about the Bible when we get to heaven, and we will relate and be with other Christians when we get to heaven; the one thing that we won't be able to do when we get to heaven is to tell other people about Jesus. Any church that does not have at least some of its energy, focus, mission, money, and strategy aimed at reaching lost people has missed part of its calling. The average evangelical church reaches about one person a year for each one hundred members; we are talking about conversions, not growth rate, which many times has nothing to do with conversions.

We sat for that first year and let our lives develop some kind of normalcy. We had a baby in the house, we had moved, our son moved out on his own for a time, my wife was being promoted at her job, but we were not doing anything at church to build relationships with anybody, and we knew that had to change. So we decided to join a small group when they began new in the fall. You have no idea how hard that was for us. How many Christians sign up for a small group with a sense of dread? This was a matter of doing what was right when you absolutely did not feel like doing it. Some would call this a bit of hypocrisy, but how many of us do things with completely perfect motives? I pray when I do not feel like it, I read the Bible when I would rather watch ESPN, I travel to far places of the world to minister to others when I would rather stay home and not risk getting some type of intestinal ailment (a little foreshadowing here). I find that if I do what is right when I do not feel like it, usually my feelings and emotions will usually catch up with me. In a fallen world, who will always feel like doing what is right? I never feel like exercising, but I try to walk every day. What I do feel like doing is reading books, watching sports on TV, eating large amounts of really bad foods, going on vacation to tropical locations and lying in the sun all day, and playing with my grandchildren instead of going to work (being self-employed has its advantages). So we joined a small group, and God was gracious to us; it was exactly what we needed at the time. We did not know then, but our church experience would begin to improve; the dark times had come to an end.

This small group was again composed of couples. It met at the home of the pastor I had known in Bible college, and the people who attended were just the right kind of group to help us ease back into church life. For one thing, this group was fun. I think that was because the pastor led the group, and he did not take himself too seriously or allow any type of format to dictate how the group would function. We had a lesson, but he kind of talked around it, let the conversation drift into other areas, and was not concerned with getting through every question. Most of the couples in the group had teenagers, and several of us were seminary or Bible college graduates, so there was a lot of commonality between us. The pastor was going through some real difficulty with one of his sons, everyone knew this, and it became an avenue for us to eventually share our experience about our daughter. I have known Christian parents who stopped going to church because of situations like this. They cannot bear the supposed shame, and they don't know how to talk to others about what happened; they feel like failures or the marriage cannot stand the strain, and they split up.

It was while we were attending this church that our daughter got married. She had met her husband through a mutual friend and after dating for a year or so decided to get married. Our son had moved out of the house to live with a close friend of his, and within a year our youngest daughter would do the same; both had found jobs and were able to support themselves. After living in a rental house for three years and attending the church for almost the same amount of time, we would suddenly become empty nesters. My wife had a long commute from our home in the suburbs to downtown, so we decided to move closer to her job and live in a high-rise apartment. This would be a huge change for us; it would be like starting over. After living for years with a rebellious child and all of the tension, drama, and suffering that this had caused us, we were suddenly released from the responsibility of having to deal with her; she was off with someone else who would have to deal with her. We were not opposed to the marriage, but we were not really for the marriage, either. We were just relieved to have a break in life, and so in response to these new circumstances, we made huge changes in how we lived.

First, we got rid of nearly everything that we owned in terms of furniture, appliances (in truth most everything we owned was pretty beat up by having so many people live with us), really anything that wasn't clothes or books. Do you perhaps see some symbolism here? Getting rid of everything we possessed sort of washed us clean of the past, as it were. We bought new furniture, found an apartment close to my wife's work on the twenty-third floor of a building that had a fantastic view of the river, mountains, and the east side of the city. It was like we were little kids; no doubt we were in some way rewarding ourselves with all of this for making it through the last decade with our marriage intact and some sort of sanity (our marriage was never really in trouble; my sanity, however, was another issue). We would look back on the two years we spent in that apartment as some of the best in our life together. She loved her job, we enjoyed living downtown, most of the time we lived there we had the place to ourselves (our youngest daughter would move in for a time), and we began to think about our relationship to church again.

We continued to go to the church in the suburbs, but it was a long drive. When we moved downtown, I think that we knew that eventually we would have to find a new church, but we did not talk about it. We were still in the sit-and-heal mode, but for me it was ending, and I wanted to do some kind of ministry. I had been involved with the local Crisis Pregnancy Center for a number of years speaking at different churches, usually during mission conferences or in January around the time of the Roe v. Wade Supreme Court decision, and I had been doing some speaking for United Way during their annual fundraising drive. I really wanted to teach, but there was not going to be any opportunity at the suburban church. I was way down the totem pole. They had seminary professors, seminary students, two pastors, and a couple of interns. So we decided to look for a new place to worship.

My wife was not thrilled because she knew I would try to find a smaller church that might have a place for me, and she knew that in a smaller church there would be no way to just sit. She still had pretty deep wounds from the cumulative effect of our mega church experience, and just did not want to leave herself open to being hurt again. In looking back, if we had had one more bad experience with a pastor or church, we might have quit going to church altogether. It took every ounce of commitment that we had to gear up and begin the search again. We had no idea where to start. We had never lived in this part of the city before; everything was new to us. The first thing that we did was to look in the Yellow Pages under churches, look under the denomination that we had the most familiarity with, and see which church was the closest. Today we would have used the Internet. Nearly every church now has a website from which you can learn much about their ministries, philosophy of ministry, vision, etc.

Let's pause for a moment to consider something that might have occurred to you as you have followed the story thus far. Would it not have been possible to reconcile with some of the pastors who caused me to leave the church that I had been attending? I should also say at this point that at those churches we did end up leaving—the second Baptist church, the Reformed church, and the mega church—our experience was usually positive until whatever the issue was that ended up being the catalyst that caused us to leave. Had we not been hurt (in the case of the second Baptist church, the mega church, and the Reformed church) or found a place to minister (as in the Bible church), we might still be at one of those churches. So the question that is before us is, Why did I have to leave? Couldn't I have worked something out?

It should also be pointed out that I was not the only one making the decision to leave. My wife was also affected by these circumstances, especially in the case of the mega church. Had she been insistent on staying at one of the churches that we left, there might have been a different outcome.

There are verses in the Bible that deal with reconciling Christians who are at odds or who have sinned against one another. Could not something have been done to fix the situation so that the rather drastic measure of leaving the church was not the end result? Well, yes and no. In each of the four churches that we left, except for the Bible church, no one made any real attempt to talk with us about how what they had done left us feeling hurt, betrayed, and injured. No one ever admitted any wrongdoing. No leader ever said, "We are so sorry this happened. What can we do to make it right?"

In the smaller churches where everyone knew who we were, almost no one ever called to find out what happened or to say that they missed us, even after we had attended these churches for years and had been involved in leadership. In the case of the mega church, our disappearance was like many who come and go in larger churches; no one really noticed. Could I have just taken the pain and learned from the situation and stayed at the churches, being the bigger man as it were (this is not to say that in any way was I more "spiritual" than someone else, probably quite the contrary)? Remember, I usually hated leaving these churches. Each time I left a church, especially the smaller ones, it caused me sleepless nights and intense personal conflict. Like everyone, I wanted to be liked and respected, and when you leave a church, those in your wake are usually (human nature being what it is) not going to think of you in the same way as when you were a member of the congregation. Perhaps that's why nobody ever called us after we left.

To use an analogy that is admittedly fraught with danger, let's think about what happens when a marriage falls apart. One spouse finds out that the other spouse has been having an affair with another person. Let's suppose everything had been going along well in the marriage up until that point (at least the one not having the affair thought things were going well). Then the truth comes out and there is the sense of betrayal, loss, pain, hurt, and perhaps the inability to believe that you will ever be able to trust or love your spouse again. Some spouses are able to forgive and reconcile, but far more end up apart, and the process to put the marriage back together can take months if not years and be a long and arduous road. The majority of couples do not make it down this road (both spouses have to want to be reconciled; sometimes one spouse has found another person so this cannot happen). So while it is possible to bring together two people who have become estranged by the actions of one, it is not common. It is so hard to look at a spouse who has been involved with someone else in the same manner as before that many times the injured party cannot find the strength or resolve (nor should they in some cases) to bring the marriage back together.

In the case of being hurt by those in leadership, it is somewhat the same. Once someone in leadership betrays you, questions your doctrinal fitness for no good reason, is so incompetent or insensitive that they cannot help you in a time of desperate need in your life, you just will not look at them the same way, certainly not as someone who is supposed to be responsible for telling you how to live your life. In each case where we ended up leaving a church because we were hurt (the second Baptist church, the Reformed church, the mega church), it was not going to be possible for me to respect the leadership of those churches or to quickly get over the feelings that accompanied each situation. Had I been a bigger person, with less pride, maybe something could have been worked out. But the point remains that no one really wanted to work anything out, so there you are.

## Principles for the Pastor

1.  *The motives those who visit and join your church.* Every church has those who visit who will become members; this is one of the main ways that churches grow in numbers. Everyone who joins a church comes with not only a set of expectations but with a history of their time in church, their baggage. Many pastors do not either inquire or care about the background of those who come to their church; the fact that they are one more body is enough. The reality, however, can be quite different. Some of those who come to a new church have caused difficulty in other churches they have attended and may bring that same behavior with them. If we are talking about a larger church, this is probably not going to be much of an issue. If the church is smaller, then the pastor may

have just inherited another pastor's problem. The best way to find out the context someone is coming from is, after a time at your church, to ask him or her about their life and church experience.

I don't recall any pastor ever asking me about my prior church experience. I suspect they either did not want to know or were afraid of what they might hear. I know that most pastors want people to join their church. Just be aware that some of them may become problems down the road. If a pastor knows this early on, it will help him to know better how to assimilate them into the congregation.

2. *The church is not a priority for many who attend.* Many people who attend church do just that, attend. They do not join a small group, they do not attend special functions, they do not make many friends, but they are there every Sunday. Every church has people like this. What should a pastor do with or for them? My advice would be to do nothing. These folks know that there are small groups, they know about your Sunday school, they know all of the special events the church has, they know the special ministries, yet they have chosen to limit their participation to Sunday morning. The reality in every church is you have people in various stages of spiritual life who show their commitment to the church in different ways. Many times they will grow in their faith and begin to show up at church programs and events they have not attended in the past. The best method of reaching the less committed in a church is to love them, acknowledge them when they attend with a personal greeting, and pray for them. A pastor should use his messages to teach on how the congregation should relate to and support the church, but do not make the mistake of equating church attendance with being more mature or spiritual. A pastor may guilt people into attending more church meetings, but this is not the same as helping them move forward in their commitment to Christ.

3. *How do you get church members to join small groups?* Most churches typically have between 20 percent to 30 percent of their members involved in some kind of small group. It will never be possible to get everyone to join a small group, so what percentage should a church aim for in terms of small-group ministry? Sixty percent seems a reasonable figure. How might this be realized? First of all, the pastor needs to be convinced of the value of attending a small group. Then he needs to have a group of leaders who have been trained to lead small groups with material that will meet the needs of those in the groups. Churches may also need different kinds of groups, groups appropriate for those in different phases of discipleship. If you put a mature believer in the same group as a new believer, you may have difficulty finding material that will meet the needs of each person. This sounds simple, but it is a formula most churches can follow.

   The pastor's job will be to train the leaders, convince the church of the value of joining a group through a series of messages on different topics relating to fellowship, care and concern for each other, intentionality, accountability, meeting needs, prayer, outreach, etc. Then the church can have a specific time (usually after a morning service) when it asks people to sign up for groups that will begin shortly. If the pastor has given good messages on how small groups can meet needs in the congregation, has trained leaders and good material, and provided a time to sign people up, he should expect at least half of his adult members to join.

4. *People who leave a church because of something the pastor has done.* Pastors will have people leave churches because of things they have said, done, or not done. Many times they will let the pastor know this. Sometimes he finds out about it after they are gone; sometimes he will never know. What should a pastor do if he finds out someone has left his church? First,

he doesn't have to do anything; once they are gone, they are not going to come back.

If a pastor learns that someone left because of him, he has nothing to lose by going and talking to them. If he has caused offense to them, he has an opportunity to clear things up. If it is a matter of vision or philosophy, he can discuss those issues. He might learn from them that what he has done has affected others as well who have not made their feelings known yet. If a pastor goes to those who have left in a spirit of humility and openness, he may not win them back, but he might be able to calm the waters and learn things about himself and the church that he did not know before. Finally, if it is required, it may be necessary to apologize and ask for forgiveness.

# Questions to Ponder

## The Priority of Church

1. How do you feel about those who only come to church for Sunday morning?

2. Why do you think some people remain on the fringe of the church and never really commit themselves?

3. What have you done to try and reach those on the fringe of the church? How successful have you been?

## Joining Small Groups

1. How does your church typically get small groups up and running? Do you go all year or take a break for the summer?

2. How important do you think it is for your members to be in a small group? How important is it to your board for members to be in small groups?

3. What are some reasons people have given for not attending small groups?

4. Does your church have a kickoff event for small groups?

5. Does your church offer different types of small groups? How do you determine the makeup of your small groups? Couples? Gender? Age? Subject? What do you think is the best way to form groups to mature your congregation?

## People Who Have Left the Church Because of Something You Have Done

1. Have you had the experience of someone leaving your church because of something you did or did not do? What were the circumstances? Did you try and remedy the situation before and/or after they left? Did you feel the reason they left was valid?

2. Do you expect that people will leave your church because of things you will do or say?

3. How fearful are you that people will leave the church because of your words or actions? Do you ever change your sermon because you know it might cause offense to someone, and they might leave?

4. Would you change your mind on an issue, project, or your philosophy of ministry if you knew a large giver to the church would leave?

5. Does your board know that it is to be expected that people may leave because of things you either do or don't do? How do they react when people leave on your account?

6. How personally do you take it when people leave the church? Has God been able to help you get a perspective on this and help you deal with the emotions involved?

# The Last Church

## Part One: Richard

So we started with the church that was closest to where we lived that was of the same denomination of the church in the suburbs. We knew that it was a small church. From the outside it looked like it could hold around two hundred or so, and there was no way that we were not going to be noticed. This would be the first time we would be looking for a church as "empty nesters," which puts you in a different category of visitor. You are not looked at as favorably as if you had children (I am being brutally honest), but by not having children and being a little older, you probably have more disposable income, which for any church is a plus. I am not saying that churches have some sort of grading system for their visitors, but don't be so naïve as to assume that a couple who visits a church who is perhaps well off (car and clothes can be a giveaway) won't be looked at differently than a college student (who will be gone in less than four years) or a single lady (this reality is addressed in James 2). Of all the churches that we eventually joined (the total to this point is six if you are keeping score), this church was the only one where the pastor visited us within a few weeks. Maybe this was because the man was just a better pastor or because of the circumstances of the church. I am only making an observation and trying not to draw any conclusions. Well, that's not exactly true; churches like people with money, so there, I have said it. It is just a reality that in our culture and society there are lots of people who make lots of money, and some of them are Christians.

Most churches seem to expect that their leadership will be composed of the most "successful" men in the church; this is in some minds an indication of God's blessing on them. The most "spiritual" man that I ever knew worked on cars for a living. He was never considered for leadership in the church he attended. Similarly, one of my best friends, an electrician, has faithfully attended his church for over twenty-five years, given faithfully, proved his commitment to Christ (at least in my mind) by being involved in the pro-life movement, and putting his entire financial future at risk; this man, too, has never been considered for leadership. So I knew when we walked into the church on Sunday morning as visitors what we might expect. I wore jeans just so people would notice that I was not conservative in my dress. Yes, I am that shallow.

When you visit a church, I think it is best to arrive just as the service is beginning (unless you have kids), so that you can get a seat without a lot of chitchat. It gives you an hour or so to get a feel for what the church is like, at least in a superficial way. You get to look the bulletin over, see what is going on at the church, experience the worship, and get an idea of the demographics and a feel for what the pastor is like. In some churches all the pastor does is the sermon; in other churches, he greets everyone, does the announcements, offers a prayer, and perhaps closes the service. It is perhaps not fair to evaluate a church based on one service, but there are some things that will turn me off every time. The most serious is irreverence, not to be confused with familiarity. Irreverence is being flippant about God or not taking Him or the Bible seriously. Familiarity is different; it means to me it is okay to be relaxed in church. It is okay to laugh in church, and it is okay to use humor during the sermon.

We sat in the back, a habit I picked up at the Bible college during chapel times so I could study during that forty-five minutes, and we were off. The service was pretty standard for a church of their size; the music was okay, but it was the pastor who got my attention. He preached using a PowerPoint presentation; this was the first time that I remember seeing the outline of the sermon put on a big screen with various illustrations as well. This is more the norm a decade or so later, but then it was still a novelty. We are now a video culture, and the church has adopted some forms of the new technology to reach a generation that carries a cell phone in one hand and an iPod in the other. He also did not have any notes that I could see. I had never seen anyone preach a message without any notes; I thought to myself, *This guy must be really smart.* He was about forty or so, very tall, and spoke easily, with little hesitation and command of his subject.

When the service was over, we stood up to see what would happen. I knew that my wife would be a little nervous and would just want to get out as soon as possible. But it was not to be. I think that we were the only visitors that day, and we had several people come up to us and introduce themselves and engage us in polite conversation. When we were asked what brought us to the church, I explained that we had recently moved downtown from the suburbs. I did not say that we were looking for a church; that is a buying signal that you may not want to share on your first visit when you are just trying to get the lay of the land. Then they did something that really made me uncomfortable: they asked if we would like to join them for lunch. What do you say to someone who invites you out for a meal whom you have known for about five minutes? You could say that you have plans, which you do because you have a plan to eat somewhere, but saying you have plans means something special that you cannot change, and we had no plans. I forget how it came about that we agreed to go out to lunch with them, but we did. There were three other couples, all about twenty to twenty-five years older than us, and they took us to a sports pub close to the church.

When you visit a church, you are only going to have about ten or so minutes for people to interrogate you, but when you sit down for a meal, you allow people to ask a number of questions about your background (Did you grow up in the city?), your family (Do you have children?), your employment (Where do you work?), your education (I went to this school. Did you go to college in this state?), and your spiritual journey (How did you become a Christian?). I was extremely uncomfortable during that meal; everyone was very polite, but I knew there was one of two things going on. They were either extremely gracious, kind people, or they felt they had a fish on the line and were trying to set the hook. The reality was that it was probably a bit of both, which is not necessarily a bad thing. There are many times in life when you only get to make one first impression, and they wanted to put the best face on their church, no problem there. I had noticed during the service that there were a lot of gray heads in the auditorium. The average age in the service was probably around forty-five to fifty, and I did not notice many kids, but it was our first visit, and I was just looking, not making any judgments or decisions. There were about one hundred people in the service, a nice number for someone seeking a place where he could find some kind of ministry.

Although every church has its own history, dynamic, traditions, and feel to it, evangelical churches have much in common. Most churches are structured in pretty much the same manner, with services on Sunday, some events at the church during the week, and some type of home groups. They mostly sing the same songs and preach from the same Bible; the pastors are educated in a relatively small number of seminaries and Bible colleges. Though evangelicalism is represented by any number of denominations, the people who make up the membership of those churches are pretty much the same, as you might expect—same hopes, same dreams, same problems, same types of families, same types of jobs, same, same, same.

And there is one other distinctive that church members in evangelical churches have in common with each other. *They hardly ever talk about Jesus.* I am not talking about the sermon, I am not talking about classes, and I am not talking about home groups. These types of structures are set up so that people have to talk about Jesus. I am talking about the unstructured times that happen in the life of a church, before and after the service, for example. In most churches, the conversation before the service is pretty brief: How are you? Have a good week? Did you hear about…? How is the family? Or that old standby, the weather. Admittedly, the time before the morning service is brief, but I seldom hear conversation that revolves around the one we are coming to worship and adore. I fully realize that there is nothing wrong with these types of conversations—it is good to recognize each other with a comment or two—but surely there must be some way to work Jesus into a greeting or brief conversation. The time after the service, when you have just spent an hour or so worshipping and listening to a message from the Bible, is more problematic, for there is less of a time constraint unless you have a roast in the oven or want to be home for the kickoff.

In most churches, the congregation will visit together in groups in the lobby or hallways and talk for a while, then gather up the kids and head on home. It is in these encounters, just after a time spent focused on "spiritual things," that you might expect people to talk about Jesus. People will talk about the sermon, the service, the weather, their jobs, their illnesses, their families, the local sports team, and the news, but I rarely hear anyone talking about Jesus or the Father. I have pondered this reality for many years and have come to some conclusions. Americans have difficulty as a culture in sharing things that are personal, and what is more personal than your relationship with the holy Trinity? This difficulty with talking about the circumstances of our lives that are personal (things like worry, anxiety, unfulfilled expectations, family problems, sins that we commit) is shown when Christians meet together to pray. I have attended different forms of prayer groups for decades, and the number-one topic is always illness, who is sick, what do they have, what is their prognosis, etc. There is nothing wrong with this, but surely it shows something about us as Christians that how we feel physically is our main priority when we gather together to pray.

It might be said that praying for the sick is also a sign of the compassion we have for those who are suffering, but people suffer from other things in life besides sickness, and many people will tell you that to suffer from depression or lack of hope or the guilt that is associated with being caught in some type of sin can be worse than any type of physical suffering. Yet these types of personal tribulations are seldom brought up in prayer groups; they are too personal, too embarrassing, and some Christians feel they are they only ones who have these types of problems and sins.

There is another possibility that exists on why there is little conversation among Christians about Jesus (think about that for a second). It may be that we have little to say about Jesus because we have little experience with Jesus. It is never good to paint with too broad a brush, but if the facts bear out your observations, what do you do?

How do you decide if you are going to go back to a church for a second visit? There were a few pros: I liked the pastor, the music was okay, the church was the right size, and people had shown an interest in us as opposed to ignoring us. Because people are different, there probably isn't a set of criteria that is universal in determining what will cause people to go back a second or third time to visit a church. If there were, I would write a book about that. Sometimes the pastor will do or say something that will drive a visitor off, never to return. I once preached a sermon (more foreshadowing) on suffering that was perhaps too intellectual and not very practical (at least some said so), and a young couple that had been visiting our church for a few Sunday never came back. One pastor that I sat under in his message used an illustration of a woman that was overweight that caused an audible gasp from the congregation. Had I been a visitor, I would never have returned; it was totally inappropriate.

As a speaker, you never know what you might say that will cause offense, but my guess is that you do not want to tell jokes about women who are overweight. People have left churches that I have attended because the messages had too much application and not enough truth, and others have left for the exact opposite reason. If the music is too loud or not loud enough, people may not visit a church again. All of this begs the question of what you want to get out of church, which is, of course, the wrong question. But churches have to deal with the reality of people's expectations, and so they structure themselves in such a way as to meet the expectations of those that they consider important. The Sunday morning service is usually the only time that the church is gathered all in one place, and each person who attends has preferences as to what type of music they want to hear, what type of "atmosphere" they expect, how the service will proceed, and what the pastor will say and how he will say it. One of the hardest jobs of the pastor and either his staff or his leadership team is how they are going to structure that morning service because how they set up that service is a declaration of the church's intention of who they are going to try and reach.

Each church will say that they have two basic groups that they are trying to deal with: those who are committed to the church (members) and those who aren't (everyone else, including visitors). The Sunday morning service is the place where both of these groups touch each other, and each group will bring different circumstances, backgrounds, expectations, and needs to that service.

There are some things that the pastor has to think about in leading the church in setting up the Sunday service. The church needs to worship God as a body. How do you do that and yet not exclude those who might be visiting who are not yet Christians? To put it another way, can an unbeliever walk into a church and not become isolated and marginalized because they have no idea of what is going on? After all, they do not know the songs, the style of music, or the special language of church, which includes many of the words in the Bible that Christians know but which may be unfamiliar to those who visit, words such as *grace, reconciliation, justification, atonement, sanctification,* etc.

If you want people to visit your church who are not Christians, you had better realize that at this point in the twenty-first century they are not going to understand a lot of what you say, so either explain it or make it simple. If you set up your service to try and make visitors who may not be Christians feel comfortable, how will this affect the fact that the members of the church need to have a corporate experience of worship? It seems that even in the early church there were people who attended the meetings of Christians (which were probably held in homes) and could understand what was going on. Paul writes about this in 1 Corinthians 14:24, 25. So it is not to be unexpected that your church will have people visit who for one reason or another feel that on that particular Sunday they need to attend church.

If your church has decided that your Sunday morning service will be one of the ways that you are going to reach out to the lost, you had better make your service something they can at least understand and find some commonality with the culture they live in. Music is the most obvious and causes the most problems for churches; it is very difficult to find music that is acceptable to different generations, if not impossible. If you want to try and reach young people, you have to have music in your worship of God that is at least in some respect like the music kids listen to on their MP3s and iPods (remember back to Calvary Chapel and how their use of music that was rock-and-roll based reached thousands of kids in the early 1970s and brought the church's song selection and worship kicking and screaming into the twentieth century).

But it is not only music that separates the church from its culture. It is also how people dress. There are still those who insist that you need to dress up when you come to church; it shows respect to God and communicates that when Christians come to worship together they really mean business and will show that in how dressed up they are. I honestly don't care how people dress for church except for this: if you have decided to make your church a place where those who do not know Christ can feel welcome and not out of place, why would you dress in a way that shows them (your visitors) they are not part of your group? Where we live, the culture is very relaxed, despite the fact that there is a Starbucks on every corner (as a non-coffee drinker, I can have some fun with those who spend $3.50 for their caffeine intake). What is some young couple going to think if they visit a church and the first person to greet them is wearing a suit from the 1950s and is twice their age? It is hard enough to get those who are not Christians to darken the doors of an evangelical church. Why make it harder by having them enter a world that not only sounds different but the people in it look different? You cannot change the content of the Bible for your visitors, you cannot change the words of the songs that you use to worship God, but you can change or modify the music to make it more relevant and common to your visitors, and you can dress in such a way as to make them feel they have not walked on to the set of *Leave It to Beaver* where the mom was always dressed in pearls and a dress.

The bigger problem, the elephant in the room, is that churches need to use the Sunday morning service as their main outreach into the community because they have no other way to reach those who are not Christians. I have already mentioned that research by George Barna and others has shown that the average evangelical church reaches about one person a year for every one hundred members, a conversion rate of 1 percent, which means that if a church is going to grow, it will need to attract those who are already Christians, which takes us back to our story. It is a fact that churches, especially leaders and the pastor, talk about those who visit their churches. Most churches encourage those who visit to fill out some kind of welcome card in case they want to contact you. My experience has been that only about a third of visitors fill out these types of cards; most know that if they fill the card out they can expect some kind of contact, and they may not be ready for that quite yet.

Churches use the information on these cards in different ways. One of the churches that we attended had a group of sweet older ladies who would visit the people who filled out the cards the next week with a bag of homemade cookies and information about the church. I thought, and still do, that this was brilliant. Everyone likes homemade cookies, and the ladies who delivered them were just there for that. There was no intention of a "visit," just an acknowledgement that they knew we were at their church and thanks for coming. If the pastor had shown up, that might be perceived as overkill, and you would be considered rude if you did not invite him in, even if your house was really messy. Even if the pastor had called first and set up an appointment, most visitors, unless they indicate on the card that they want the pastor to visit (either a buying signal that they are looking for a church or an indication that they are looking for something else—go with caution) do not want this level of communication; it is too personal and too intimate for a one-time visit to a church. I must have filled out a card during our first visit, and the pastor called soon thereafter and asked if he could come by and see us. Since there were things that I wanted to know about the church, we arranged for him to come by on a weekday evening after dinner.

You have to remember that we had just moved into this penthouse apartment in a secure building in downtown. It was quite the place, with spectacular views of the mountains to the east and the river right below us. The only problem with the apartment was that it was on the twenty-third floor, and I had a real problem with heights. It shows how much I love my wife that I agreed to live there. I rarely went out on the deck, and when I did, if I looked over the edge toward the ground, I felt like I wanted to throw myself off—this besides the fact that I got dizzy and my heart pounded. This period in my life coincided with the fact that for four years, due to my fear of heights and a certain type of vertigo, I was unable to drive across most of the bridges in the city, which caused a certain amount of inconvenience for those who had to drive with me. My best friend and I had been surfing for a number of years, and when it was my turn to drive, I avoided the bridge that was the quickest way to the beach and took a longer route that did not cause me the panic, sweaty palms, and heart palpitations that going over the high bridge did. After a number of years, he finally got tired of this, and one day coming back from the coast just said, "Go over the stupid bridge. You can do this." I don't know what he was thinking. Having never suffered from any type of phobia himself, he did not know what he was dealing with. I mean, he was taking his life in his hands, but I made it over the bridge, not without the usual symptoms, but I made it nonetheless. From that day to now, I have been able to cross most bridges with only minor discomfort, except for the Richmond Bridge over the backwater of San Francisco bay; I did it once and will never do it again.

So the pastor came by to visit. His name was Richard, and he had been at the church for a number of years, first as the youth pastor and then as the pastor when the previous man left for another church. I don't know what he thought during the visit, but afterward, he knew that I was a Bible college graduate, we were looking for a place to serve, that we both worked, and that our children all lived in the area. At that point my wife was on her way up the corporate ladder and would be promoted to vice president. I still had my distribution business, but because I had good people working for me, I only actually worked about twenty-five hours a week. The pastor was working on his doctorate from a prominent evangelical seminary and seemed pretty normal to me. It was hard to make judgments based on one visit, but there was nothing in the visit that was going to turn us away from the church.

He mentioned that the church was just completing a course in some kind of church renewal, which they had been involved in for two years. He was confident that the church would find renewed vision and growth when they completely implemented the changes that they were working on. He asked if I would like to attend a meeting to see what this was all about. Well, in for a penny, in for a pound. I had no idea how attending this meeting would affect my future; such are the ways of God with His children. You go to a church because it is the closest to where you live, you are visited by the pastor (something we would discover later that he hardly ever did), and you are invited to a meeting that you could have said no to because you were just beginning to attend. You never know what events or circumstances God will use to shape your future and those around you.

There were some good reasons for us not to attend this church. It had hardly any young people. It was about fifty years old, which meant it was probably pretty traditional, conservative, and would have a set way of doing things. There were some nontraditional churches that we could have looked at, but for some reason that I cannot remember, we chose to stay with a more traditional type of church. Although this church was a member of the denomination that had a seminary in town, there were no seminary students attending the church, nor were there any college students from the other colleges in the area.

It turned out that the church was just about ready to put in place some of the changes that they had been learning about in their ongoing church renewal seminar. The meeting that the pastor had invited me to was about the new format they were going to adopt. They would add a new structure that in a few months would replace the two existing adult classes and, more importantly, change the times of the service and the adult classes. The service would be held first, at 9.30 a.m., followed by the adult class. This would be a pretty big change for the church. There were thoughts that some of the people would not come to a 9:30 a.m. service, but this was what the church consultant had pitched to them, and they were going to do it come hell or high water. In most churches, the adult classes are before the service, although in larger churches these types of classes can be before, after, or even during the worship service if there is more than one service. When the adult classes are before the worship service, it gives people the option to opt out of these classes and still attend the service. By putting the worship service first and the classes afterward, the thought was that you would increase the number of people who would attend the adult class because they were already at church. But that class had better have something to offer, or they might just go home.

So Richard had a lot riding on this class, and he and the leadership team were taking great pains to do this right. They had a number of meetings with the congregation to communicate the changes they were proposing, letting people give their input and comments, but there was no doubt about what direction they were going to pursue. The church had been in decline for a number of years and needed to be reinvigorated, renewed, and reenergized. The church renewal seminar that they had participated in had a great reputation for helping churches to establish a process in their church to make disciples and move people along in their spiritual journey. One piece of this process was to have middle-size classes (from twenty to seventy people) right after the morning service that would serve to not only teach the Bible but to assimilate new people into the church. This class would have snacks, an opening that would be different each week, and have several people involved in leadership: a teacher, a host, a coordinator for special events, and an outreach leader. The class would host several events a year outside of the church that class members could invite friends to (golf, bowling, etc.) There was only one problem: there wasn't anyone in the church who was really qualified to be the teacher.

The teacher was just one part of the team who would lead the class, but this person had the most face time and needed to possess not only the ability to teach but to interact with the class, as well. They did not want the teaching time to be another message that was similar to the sermon they had just heard in the service. The idea was to teach a lesson but have built into it questions, interaction, and a measure of fun. Since there would be people who were at different stages of their Christian lives (and some who might not be Christians at all), the teaching time needed to be simple, understandable, and have some type of application. The meeting that I attended was designed to start putting these pieces together, and as I met with this group, it became obvious that there wasn't anyone who had the qualifications to teach this type of class, unless it would the pastor.

It is interesting to think again about the timing that God orchestrates in our lives. If we had waited just one month to begin attending the church, the process of beginning that class would have been pretty far along, and I would not have been invited to the meeting that was putting the class together. Everyone's life has moments like this, when something happens that has little significance at the moment, but later you realize how important the timing of the circumstance was and how your life would have been different had the timing been different. To bring this loop of the story to an end, I became the teacher of that class and would continue in that role for almost a decade.

Richard and the leadership team were determined to bring about these changes in the church in a manner that would guarantee success. Bringing change of any type to a traditional church is difficult and fraught with danger. The previous pastor years earlier had attended a seminar on contemporary worship with a number of people from the church and the next Sunday, literally the next Sunday, completely changed the worship style without letting anyone know what was coming, and about a third of the church walked out during the service. This memory was still fresh in many people's minds, so there was a concerted effort to have a number of meetings with the congregation to explain why the church was moving a new direction, what they thought would result from the changes, and how the changes would affect the ministry of the church. It was not only the service and adult class that would be new, but the small group ministry of the church would also be restructured according to a new model that was part of the church renewal seminar (more on this later).

Which brings us to the whole topic of change. By and large, traditional, conservative evangelical churches do not like change. They do not seem to mind changing pastors, but they do not like changing the structure or atmosphere or philosophy of the church. By structure, I mean things like the worship service. Try changing the order of the worship service and see what happens, like putting the message in the middle of the service. People become used to routine, and if you change the routine, it can make a lot of the congregation uncomfortable. Many Christians have a set of expectations when they come to church, especially with regard to the worship service, and if these expectations are not met, they do not feel right. If people come to church and do not have the emotional feeling from the service that they expect, someone is going to hear about it, especially if that lack of emotional response is directly related to some change in the structure of the church.

This church was going to change nearly everything, so they had to be careful. It was a tribute to the church renewal seminar process that they were involved in that the change (moving the service time, adding two new classes that would be after the service instead of before, and having to adjust the kids' ministry to match the new worship times) was accomplished without a lot of drama. That this happened relatively smoothly was due to the amount of time and communication the leadership put into bringing about these changes. That does not mean that everyone was in agreement or that there wasn't grumbling about the changes. It is just not possible to bring about a radical change in the structure of a traditional evangelical church without some sort of dissension, even if you do everything according to your plan and communicate to everyone what you are going to do and the reasons for the change. There are just some people who will be against whatever the pastor and the leadership team want to do, for a variety of reasons. Some people feel they are smarter than the pastor; some people who are not in leadership (and probably should not be in leadership) will want to oppose leadership just to either get noticed or have a feeling of control; some people view any change as the pathway to liberalism and a departure from the truth.

Richard had staked everything on the process that they had learned from the church renewal seminar, and if it did not work, it would probably signal the end of his ministry. The church had been sliding down for many years, from a high of about 350 to about 125, and I know that he felt that the status quo just was not an option. He did a good job of leading the team right up to the point of bringing all this change about, and it would remain to be seen if these changes could start the church on a road to renewal.

The first Sunday succeeded exactly as he had hoped. The worship service went off without a hitch at the new hour of 9:30 a.m., and there was no noticeable drop in attendance. It would turn out that some of the older members were only able physically to make it to one service, and some of them chose to come to the new class after the worship service. One of the results of changing the service times and having the adult classes after the service was that we consistently had more people in the second hour than the first hour, something of an oddity for an evangelical church. Most churches have fewer people attend their adult classes than the worship service, but in our case, it would be just the opposite. Some of this was due to the timing of the service and the classes, but some of it was also how the adult classes were structured. Of the two adult classes that we had, one was for ages twenty to sixty and one for retirees (you have to remember we were a small church; normally you would not have a class with such a broad age range as twenty to sixty).

We were also hampered in that we really only had one person to teach the younger class, and that was me. No one had really heard me teach before, but I had been in the group that brought all of this together, and I had expressed some ideas on how the teaching part of the class might be done. The class was about seventy-five minutes long, and besides, the teaching part had an opening, a recurring prayer time every other week, and some type of interaction in the class led by the class leader.

The class leader was supposed to be the real head of the class, not the teacher, but it would not work out that way for the first several months. Since the teacher had the most face time, it was hard not to view the teacher as the "leader" of the class, not just one of the team. I suppose this is natural, but we wanted to keep the class from becoming a teacher-dominated time. The thought was to make this class as much fun as possible, with a lot of participation by the class in every part, including the teaching. I decided to teach different topics, each one lasting a month, so that we would have a lot of variety and be on to something new every few weeks. I wanted to have the class involved in the teaching time, so I gave out a handout each week, with blanks to fill out that related to things that I would cover in the lesson. If you filled out every blank there would be a prize for you at the end of the class. These prizes went from the sublime to the ridiculous, including Christian books, candy, comic books, any number of items from the Dollar Store, etc. It turned out to be a real hit—it kept people involved in the lesson, the class ended on a fun note as people came forward to get their prizes, and it caused a lot of laughter as people reached into the large bag to pull out their prize. The giving out of prizes eventually became somewhat of a liability as people became too focused on filling out the answers and not really listening to the content of the lesson, but for months it worked well and brought about the tone we wanted in the class.

It is good to remember that I had not been involved in any kind of ministry for years and at the time the class began was forty-eight years old. My whole ministry experience up to this time consisted of teaching a class for a few months at the Reformed Church and leading a couple of small groups. I had a lot of experience speaking before people (Crisis Pregnancy Center, United Way) but not so much in a church context. I had been at the church less than a year when the class began. The pastor was taking a bit of a chance letting me teach the new class that was part of the process of renewal without really knowing how I would do, but sometimes in ministry (and life) you have to take risks and see what happens.

One of the dynamics that helped the class work was just the fact that I was a new person who wanted to be involved in some type of ministry. The core group of the church had not changed in many years, and those available for ministry knew each other really well, and just by being a new and unknown quantity, it gave the class a different feel than had the pastor or someone else been the teacher. The class started out with about forty people and would grow steadily for the next several years and brought a real sense of renewal to a group that had gotten pretty beat down as they watched the church steadily decline.

In addition to setting up the adult class and reversing the order of the service, one of the things that the church renewal seminar focused on was how to structure and organize small groups. The church had a number of small groups, but they were all organized differently and had no common purpose or goal. Some had leaders; some were just a collection of friends and were more of a support group than small Bible study group. No one had given these groups any attention for years, and they just sort of continued on and on. The church renewal seminar wanted each church to have three types of groups: one for outreach, one to teach habits, and one to teach character. You attended the group that matched where you were at in your spiritual journey and used appropriate material for that group. Richard had started an outreach group with another elder and was in the process of beginning a small group that would focus on developing the habits of the Christian life—things like prayer, fellowship, giving, service, Bible reading, witnessing, and commitment. It would turn out that the church (and the pastor in particular) would not be able to bring this change about, though there was a lot of effort put into trying to make the change. The reality was that people did not mind changing the service times and the structure of the adult classes, but some proved to be resistant to changing the way they met for small groups. It was also easier to manage the change of one structure (the adult class) because everyone could be there at the same time, whereas you can only be in one small group at a time.

With an adult class, you only have one teacher and a few other leaders. With six different small groups going, you have to get a much larger number of people to agree to change the way they do things, train them in how to lead the specific type of small group they will attend, have them become familiar with the material they will use, help them learn how to move the people in their groups forward in their spiritual lives, how to measure their progress, and how to help them if they are not progressing. It was a much more complicated process than the other changes we had done. The church renewal seminar had developed a complete process for this type of change to their form of small groups, but the pastor just could not get the leaders of the existing groups to buy into this change. His greatest difficulty was that he could not get people to see that just meeting together was not enough. You needed a plan, goals, and material to accomplish the plan and the goals and a way to measure spiritual progress. The plan that the church renewal seminar offered was based on the way that Jesus taught and dealt with His disciples and was not that difficult to set up, but it just did not happen. Many of the groups had been together for years and liked the dynamic and fellowship they currently had and saw no need to change either the structure or the content of their groups. The pastor met with these leaders but made no headway and eventually gave up. Not a good sign. It was the first time that I would witness what would be Richard's biggest failing; he just could not lead people and get them to follow where he wanted to go.

The best thing he could have done at this point was to say, "If your group isn't going to be one of the models that we have learned about at our seminar, you will not be allowed to have it promoted by the church." By allowing people to continue what they want to do, you cede to them leadership in that area of the church, and you may not get it back. Because the pushback he got was pretty strong, he decided to just let the existing groups keep doing what they wanted, and any new groups that formed would be on the new model. That was okay, but he basically told a large group in the church that they could operate outside of what the leadership had agreed would be the model of the church concerning small groups. Had he drawn a line in the sand and said, "My way or the highway," he would have won because the elder board was behind him and would have demonstrated that he was serious about renewing the church. But because he caved, this section of the church would never let him lead them. One of the reasons for this was that Richard had been at the church since he was a student at the seminary and had been promoted from youth pastor to pastor when he was still pretty young. I found out much later that the elder board told him that all he had to do was preach; they would take care of everything else.

This was a recipe for disaster, and had Richard bothered to ask one of his seminary professors if this was a good idea, they would have told him to run away as fast as he could. The elder board did not mind him being the pastor; they just did not want him as their leader. This situation unfortunately was made worse by the fact that Richard was, by his own admission, extremely introverted. As we spent more time at the church, we began to notice that he was just not a people person and had difficulty in conversing with people on any level other than the superficial. If you are the pastor of a large church, I suppose you could be an introvert since you would have a large staff to deal with people and their issues, but in a small church, it is a real handicap. The elder board knew this when they hired him and basically told him they would deal with the people issues and he could just teach and preach.

This type of arrangement will never work; it is the pastor to whom the church will look for vision, strategy, and leadership, not any type of board. It is the pastor who has the training, it is the pastor who gets a paycheck, and it is the pastor who is the face of the church. If you only hire a pastor to teach, you might as well use videos of famous preachers; it would save a lot of money. The board, probably without knowing it, handicapped the pastor at the beginning and almost certainly guaranteed that he would fail. Had Richard not been so introverted and unable to deal with people authentically and forcefully, he might have been able to overcome this arrangement with the board over time, but it was not to be.

This was not to say the he did not have a number of strengths. He was a person of great integrity, a good Bible teacher, and was as honest as the day was long. When the previous pastor left and the board was engaged in the search for a new pastor, one of the reasons they chose him was the quality of the men that they looked at. After looking at a number of candidates whose collective shortcomings made them think they might not ever find anyone qualified, they took what they knew. They knew that Richard was a decent, honest, humble, and spiritual man, though he was not a people person. They decided to get around that by offering him the job but not the position. By this, I mean he could be the teacher but pastor in name only. Ultimately, this would come back to bite the church because he chose to renew the church through the church renewal seminar but did not have the skills to carry it out completely. The first indication of this was his inability to get the small groups to change into the new model.

There were a couple of other staff members, a youth pastor and a secretary. The youth pastor would leave for seminary within a year of our joining the church, but the church secretary would serve at the church for almost twenty years. Technically she was the pastor's secretary, not the church secretary, and for the first few years we attended, she worked full time. It would turn out that she did virtually nothing; she was there mainly to answer the phone and be a presence at the church. No one really knew this at the time; the church had always had a secretary, so that was that. When she ended up leaving the church years later, it was discovered that the phone hardly ever rang, and what she did for eight hours a day was a mystery. I think she mainly served as a touch point for the elderly people (many of whom were not able to attend for physical reasons); they would call her to find out what was going on at the church. She was a very pleasant lady but would inexplicably be absent from church on many Sundays. I have no idea what she did for the pastor. She had no computer skills, he had few appointments at the church, but he jealously guarded her time and would not let other leaders in the church use her services even though she obviously had the time. It was the one area where he did draw a line and did not back down, and people learned not to ask her for favors, such as copying lessons for kids' classes or asking for a specific report (like the minutes of an annual meeting).

After the current youth pastor left, the church needed to replace him and began a search for someone new. Well, a kind of search. One of the elders had a son who had recently moved back to the city and had some kind of experience working with kids in another part of the country, though not in a church context. He had grown up in the church and in high school had gotten a girl pregnant (terrible phrase, it sounds like the girl had nothing to do with it) and left the church under a bit of a cloud. That was many years ago. He had married and had two children of middle-school age and was brought before the church as a candidate.

I look back on this incident with really mixed feelings. There was no way that he would have been offered the position had his dad not been on the elder board and a large giver to the church. I am sure Richard had reservations about him (if he didn't, he was absolutely clueless as to human behavior) but did not express them with enough force to derail the process. What the other elders were thinking, I have no idea; he had no education (not even a high school graduate; this would not necessarily matter to me, but they had never considered a candidate for that position who was not a college graduate or seminary student) and, to put it mildly, was a tad abrasive and egotistical. These qualities would not become apparent to me until later, but what I saw when he was brought before the church caused me concern. For one thing, he was too old for the position. Though he had young kids, he was not a young person, either in outlook or age. I suppose you can be a youth pastor if you are in your midthirties, but you should at least be able to relate to kids on their level. No youth minister is going to stay in the position for more than a few years; that's why most churches end up with younger men who are students or have just finished school and need a chance to learn how to do some kind of ministry. He had really nothing going for him except that his dad wanted him to have the job, and by this I mean he needed a job.

Now you might think, *How can a man with a family live on a youth pastor's salary, especially in a small church?* Well, the church had one factor that made it possible for it to have a youth pastor and pay him a living wage: the church owned a house adjacent to the property that was included in the package. When you count the rent and the utilities with the salary he was offered, he ended up making around $40,000 a year to manage around thirteen kids. He would teach Sunday school, have a youth night once a week, do some events, but that was about it, and he would be hired as a full-time position. The one reality about youth ministry is that kids are in school most of the time, have homework, and can only be worked with for a few hours a week, unless you meet with them individually. I have never run across another church that had a full-time youth minister for thirteen kids; few churches will even pay for a part-time youth minister for this size of a group. By offering him a position that guaranteed him a lot of free time with few responsibilities to take up that time, it was setting him up for problems that an experienced pastor or board might have seen.

At the meeting where he was offered as a candidate (his name was Michael), he stood up before the church and answered questions from the congregation. I had only been at the church for about a year and was watching how this meeting was going. I had some real reservations about the man but did not feel it was my place to try and make the guy possibly look bad by asking questions that he might have difficulty answering. I was mildly shocked when one of the older folks did ask him about his tattoo and hair in a gracious and inoffensive manner. He answered that the ponytail was similar to Samson's; it was to remind him of God's strength. The tattoo, which was of the Bible with a sword through it, was to remind him of the power of God's Word. No one asked him any follow-up questions, though I was tempted. I wanted to ask him why he needed physical reminders of who God is and what He had done. Why not wear a cross? Why not a tattoo on his forehead backward so when he looked in the mirror he was reminded of how much God loved him? Why not wear sandals and a robe like Jesus? You get the idea. This was so shallow; it also said to the rest of us, "I am doing something that you are not that is reminding me of God. This makes me more spiritual than you."

Michael was also a charismatic. This was even more disturbing to me, not because he was a charismatic but because the church was decidedly not charismatic. Those of the charismatic persuasion have a different way of looking at life than non-charismatics (the theological word for non-charismatic is *cessationist*), especially in terms of how the "Christian life" is lived. In nearly every other area of biblical interpretation (God, Bible, Jesus, man, sin, church), they are indistinguishable from other evangelical churches. But in the area of sanctification (how a Christian goes about living the "Christian life"), there are large differences, and most of these center on how you view the ministry of the Holy Spirit. Michael believed in the baptism of the Holy Spirit with the outward manifestation of speaking in tongues and in the direct communication of God with people, as in, "God said to me that…" Some charismatics also believe in complete sanctification, that it is possible to become free from sin. Our church did not believe any of these things and in hiring Michael was going to put him in the position of being the only one in the church who had these beliefs. Had he an incredible amount of grace and wisdom he might have been able to work in a cessationist church, but such was not the case. From the beginning, this was a situation that was not going to end well.

There were problems right from the start. Michael just did not like being a youth pastor, and it was obvious to anyone who was looking that he felt the work was beneath him. I mean, he was in his midthirties and was doing a job that in most churches our size would be done by either volunteers or a part-time person who would be much younger. I believe that he took the job mainly for the salary and the house that came with the position, which would explain his attitude toward his work. Because his dad was on the elder board and had helped him get the job, I think he felt a certain freedom to just do what he wanted. Richard was responsible for his work schedule and gave him certain other tasks outside of youth work to occupy his time, but Michael seldom did them on time or with any obvious diligence. There was talk of making him an associate pastor rather than the youth pastor, but this never happened because he could not do the work assigned to him as youth pastor in a satisfactory manner. Richard after a time just gave up on him and left him to his youth duties; it just wasn't worth the pastor's time to beat a dead horse, so to speak.

To anyone who was paying attention, this situation could not go on forever. I was not in leadership and was involved in teaching the adult class, so I did not know of this until after he was gone. I did try to stay away from him. I was afraid if I got involved in a conversation with him I might say something that I might regret. Besides the fact that he never should have been hired, the church was also much too slow in letting him go. The few times that Michael was allowed to preach were disasters. He had great difficulty in putting together coherent thoughts that related to the passage he was teaching from and was not shy about putting his charismatic beliefs into his messages. He began to step over the line when he began suggesting to various people that being the youth pastor was not what he felt called to do at the church. What he believed he felt God calling him to do at the church was to be the senior pastor. This, of course, created two problems for the leadership. The first one was that we already had a senior pastor. The second one was, how do you deal with someone who feels that the God of the universe has specifically said to them they are to be the pastor of the church?

I have only one experience of God speaking clearly to me in my life. It was either a voice, or I experienced His voice so clearly it seemed audible. I was struggling with the fact that my children at that time (teenage years) seemed to have no heart for God. I was out walking and told God that I would give my life right then and there if He would help my kids find Him. He clearly said to me, "I have already done that" (I believe that this was in reference to Jesus dying for them). Today all my kids follow Christ, but it did not happen for them until they were adults.

So the elder board began to have serious doubts about Michael and brought him to a meeting to try and work things out. It is difficult, however, to try and work things out with someone who feels that they have not only done no wrong but that you are standing in the way of him being the pastor of the church (it apparently never entered his mind that there was no way that he would ever get a majority of the votes needed to become pastor, but thinking logically wasn't his strong point). The church as a whole knew nothing about this. His dismissal would take over six months to accomplish and would come as a surprise to most of us.

It was his dad who held up his dismissal. The elder board met many times to discuss the situation, and the father was adamant that his son should not be fired, even though it was obvious he was a lousy employee and was operating outside of any kind of reporting arrangement. The other members of the board, including the pastor, just would not take the steps required to dismiss the youth pastor. Their meetings became more contentious and there was no foreseeable end in sight. It was at this point that the church elected another elder, a man who had attended the church his whole life and was well respected by nearly everyone. His name was Charles, and he knew of the situation, but when he came on the board, he was shocked to see how divided the board was. Well, not really divided—there was one man who wanted to keep the youth pastor (his dad) and three including the pastor who wanted to let him go. With the Charles's help, they were finally able to come to a resolution and let the youth pastor go. It turned out that the youth pastor's dad was mostly concerned about his son's ability to find another job and did not really disagree with his son's performance; he just wanted to keep giving him chance after chance. He was right to worry about his son's future employment—he would be out of work for nearly a year, a year in which his marriage also fell apart. He and his wife would divorce soon after they left the church.

In the end, the elder did not leave the church and, though he had behaved badly, would learn from this lesson and become a better person. The way that he learned to become a better person arrived soon after his son had left, at the next annual church business meeting. His term as elder was up, and the board put him up again for election. This was a big mistake on their part: he had subverted the will of the majority for months, had ignored the facts of his son's behavior (reinforcing the phrase that blood is thicker than water), and caused harm to the church by letting someone continue in a role that they were obviously not suited for. I don't think it occurred to the elders to not put him up. He had been an elder for years and had been elected every time. It would turn out that no one could remember a time when an elder had been presented to the church and had not been elected. But there is a first time for everything. No one at the church except the elder board was supposed to know what had transpired in their meetings, but word had gotten around about how he had tried to keep his son employed though all the elders and his son's dismal performance worked against keeping him.

I expect that the elders had told their wives of what was going on for those six months. How could you not help telling your spouse something that was eating you up inside? I am sure each elder told his wife, "You can't tell anybody about this but…" Sometimes I think the worst thing you can do is to tell someone that they must not tell somebody something that you are sharing in confidence; it's like telling a teenager not to have sex but leaving condoms lying all around. Anyway, I have found that there are few really well-kept secrets in a small church, and I was surprised at how well this one was kept. After the votes were counted, we were not immediately told in the meeting that the elder did not get enough votes to be reelected. Since the usual practice was to announce that everyone had been elected to the office that they were filling, when nothing happened, I asked the moderator, just as a matter of chance, what had happened. He said that the elder had not been reelected but they were not sure how to announce it; they did not want to embarrass him in front of the church. When it was revealed that he was not elected, I think that most people understood that it was because of his son, but they did not know the whole story, and most don't to this day.

In most cases, this would have caused the elder to either leave the church or at least cause some sort of commotion. Most men do not take this type of rejection well. Though he had displayed an obstinate streak regarding something that everyone else could clearly see, that episode did not completely define his character. We are all like this. We have good times and bad times, we succeed at some tests and fail at others, and none of us should be quick to judge someone else based on one incident or test. I feel that his true character showed in how he handled himself after the incident, taking the rejection with grace and humility and continuing on in the church. Probably one of the reasons that incident happened at all was that Richard just did not step up to the plate and show some leadership on the matter, but then the man was at that time one of the biggest givers to the church, and I believe that Richard's wife had put into his head that the worst thing that could happen to him was to get fired and lose that part of their income, so he let the thing drag on forever.

What do I say about the pastor's wife? A walking cauldron of contradictions, a whirlwind of activity who never appeared to slow down, someone whom I never saw eat a morsel of food (though the church had buffets centered around meetings all the time), a woman who constantly complained about her weight though a strong wind would knock her down (imagine the effect of complaining about your weight to women who actually were overweight), a woman who put impossible pressure on her kids to succeed at school, a person who loved kids and would watch people's children for a weekend so they could get away, a woman who would casually swear just to let you know that she was not a prude, who gossiped about other people in the church so frequently that I actually avoided her most of the time, someone who had difficulty forgiving anyone who either said anything that she might consider negative about her husband or offered him advice on church affairs, who believed that it was the elders who were keeping him from succeeding (Do I sound petty? I don't mean to be.) and who would end up driving many of the church family away from her for some of the reasons listed above. When we first came to the church, she made a point of introducing herself but did not mention that she was the pastor's wife. I found out later that she never introduced herself as the pastor's wife; she had her own identity and did not under any circumstance want to be thought of as somebody's anything. She had her own career and a huge network of friends in the business world and loved to drop names of well-known people in the city she rubbed shoulders with or happened to be in meetings with.

She also had multiple sclerosis, and though she had the type that could be in remission for long periods of time, it helped define her in a way that chronic diseases can sometimes do. Her father had been a pastor, and my guess is that there was measure of rebellion from the whole lifestyle that pastor's kids sometimes get caught up in (say the right thing, act the right way, be respectful to everyone, don't run in church—that sort of thing). She was such the opposite of her husband, who was introverted to the point of disability; I wondered many times how they managed to function together as a couple. Except for their kids, it seemed like they lived separate lives. As she watched the church decline under her husband's time as pastor and his time at the church began to draw to an end, she became increasingly blunt and vocal in her opinions because she knew that she was getting out. This created a huge conflict in her; she did not want to leave the city and her network of friends, the career she had, the schools her kids attended, all because her husband could not get the church to grow. This did not seem fair to her. I think this contributed to her increasing unhappiness over the last months, and I felt for her. I hate to see people unhappy due to circumstances that they have no real control over, but what are you going to do? She was supposedly a mature believer, but like I said before, we don't always act according to our better natures in every test or incident in our lives.

You may be thinking at this point, *I thought the church was in a time of renewal. Wasn't that the whole point of attending the church renewal seminar?* You would be correct. That was the whole point of the church renewal seminar, but to get the results, you have to put the pieces in place, and in that, the church failed. The church did manage to change the order of the service and put in the classes that came after them, but the church did not manage to put in to place two other crucial pieces that were vital to renewal and becoming relevant again. One of the pieces was outreach small groups, where you invite friends and neighbors to a study about the life of Christ, with the thought that some of them would become believers. Richard did manage to get one group going, but it lasted six months, and no one became a Christian, though everyone had a good time. Because Richard was generally not a people person, he was probably not the person to lead such a group, but at least he tried, which was something. There wasn't anyone who really had a burden to do this, so this piece just died. The best person to lead this type of group, in hindsight, would have been the pastor's wife, but I don't think that was ever considered.

The other piece that never got up and running was the other type of small group, one that concentrated on discipleship. The church had a number of small groups, but they had no real idea of what they were trying to accomplish (most groups began each new year with the question, What do you want to study this year?) and were not set up based on age, life experience, or anything else that made sense. When Richard tried to get these groups to use the model that the church renewal seminar proposed, he met real resistance along the lines of "We have always done it this way" (I am not kidding, people actually used that exact phrase). He held a few meetings with the small group leaders, suggesting material, going over why the new model was better (it used things like accountability and intentionality that were not practiced in the current groups) and how everyone should be on the same page when it came to ministry. He failed miserably. He just could not get this piece put in place, and that was that. People liked to meet with each other and study the Bible, but they did not want to put the work into the new model, work they thought was not necessary. It was after this that I believe that Richard knew that he would not be able to change the culture of the church (though he would give it one more try a few years later), and he resigned himself to a measure of failure, which caused him to become even more withdrawn into himself.

Compounding this, Richard's father was a demanding man who expected his son to become some sort of professional (his hope was that he would become a lawyer), and when the son decided to go into the ministry, he incurred the silent but nonetheless real wrath of his dad. Because he let his dad down and because his dad rode him pretty hard most of his life, it left Richard pretty fragile and insecure, and to compensate he held himself to nearly impossible standards of performance and spirituality that left him constantly disappointed in himself because he could not reach these levels of perfection. He made mention of the effect that his dad had on him in some of his messages, so he realized how his dad had shaped his view of himself and much of his character, but he could not break free of these chains, and it was painfully obvious to many of us in the church that this was a millstone around his neck, influencing his ministry and his own happiness. To my regret, after a while, I just gave up trying to get close to him and be his friend. I just didn't think that was going to ever happen. I never did have an honest talk with him about what I saw in his personality. I never said to him, "How can I be your friend?" I never said to him, "How can I help you be successful?" I just gave up. It wasn't until several years later that I finally went to him and told him what I had been seeing for all those years, but it was too late; he was halfway out the door.

Have you noticed that, so far, nothing bad has happened to us at this church? At this point, we had been there several years, and it had been uniformly a great experience. I had been able to find a teaching ministry that fit my gifts and abilities; we had been accepted into the church pretty seamlessly; there would be people in the church who would become our good friends, and I had been given the opportunity to teach on a regular basis overseas and have an impact in other cultures. Some of this was because the church we had landed at was pretty mature, and though it was composed of sinners just like every other church, the people had a reservoir of grace and selflessness.

I also think that God had allowed us to go through the previous church experiences to refine our character, learn certain things about people and how churches work, and that our identity does not depend on what we do but rather who we are in Christ. Because I really did not begin any significant ministry until later in life, I never developed any sort of identity that I was a teacher or pastor or elder or leader or anything that related to something that I did in the Christian world. My job certainly provided no sense of identity or purpose. For the most part, I did the job as well as I could, but there was no career path, no chance for advancement, and no way to make any more money by working harder or longer. Through all of the difficulties that we had gone through, both of us had developed a faith that was strong, centered on what Christ had done for us and who He was to us. Many pastors and Christian leaders find much of their identity and meaning in their positions, leaving them at the mercy of their circumstances and subtly viewing those who do not have positions of leadership as less spiritual. There was one elder at the church in particular (Charles) who almost could not function without being an elder. Much of his life revolved around managing the details of the church and being on the elder board. He was a gracious and kind man but found too much of his meaning in life being an elder and not enough in just being a Christian.

The church's one main drawback was its elder board and how it was structured. I have already mentioned how the elder board told the pastor when he was hired that all he had to do was preach. They would manage the church and deal with most every other issue that came up. This was fine in theory, but in practice it was the pastor who was at the church every day, not the board, and over time this arrangement just would not work. People wanted the pastor to be the leader (why else would we be paying him?), and the board could not go to the church and say, "We are the real leaders of the church. Look to us for leadership and management." So there was this uneasy relationship between the board and Richard. He wanted to lead but was by temperament not able to do so; the board wanted to lead but was practically unable to. The board was led by a chairman who ran the board meetings and set the agenda, another structural oddity that handicapped the pastor, who was just a participant and in no way a leader or visionary.

The two men who were the chairmen for decades were good men but knew of the weaknesses of the pastor and did not ever try to help him develop into a leader by either giving him the chance to lead or encouraging him to take more control of church affairs, etc. Had they come up with a plan, including a timetable, to help him develop into the leader of the church and given him the authority and support to be the pastor in the fullest sense of the word, things might have been substantially different. They met nearly every week even if there were no real issues to discuss, which also reinforced the idea that the pastor was just a paid employee and not the leader of the church. One of the chairmen would eventually move away, and Charles assumed the role of chairman but would not last long in that position, for reasons that he could not have foreseen.

There was another problem with the elder board, one that they could not help. None of them had ever attended another church, so they had no other perspective or experience to draw from when they thought about church. It is in some ways commendable to stay at one church through thick and thin (think of my experience and how we did not like changing churches), but it can also breed a lack of curiosity about how things are done at other churches. To compound this, they were by nature not curious men. Between them they had not read one book on church renewal, church leadership, church movements, church structure, or church philosophy and ministry. They did not know about the emerging church and the effect it was having on the traditional evangelical church, nor did they know any of the seismic changes that were happening in the world of evangelical theology (open theism, universalism, denial of hell), something elders are specifically commanded to know. What they did know was the history of that church, and they all had been there when the church had over four hundred people attending, and when the church renewal seminar did not bring those hundreds of people back to the church (though it did revitalize the church and bring in some new people, particularly younger people), they began to get antsy.

Richard attended various ministerial functions during the year, and it was at one of these functions that he met several pastors from a relatively new emergent church. They had been growing at a phenomenal rate and had several churches in the metro area. They were on the cutting edge technologically and were reaching large numbers of people who had never attended church before. They had a church plant going in the downtown area but were not happy with the location and were looking for another. Richard began talks with them that he would continue with the elder board along the lines that we could offer them our church Saturday evenings or Sunday afternoon for their service (at that point, they were not locked into a Sunday morning format), and we could learn from them how they managed to have a more relevant worship service and reach the lost. He brought the pastors to the elder board, and we began to discuss how this partnership might work. You will perhaps notice that I used the word *we* when I mentioned the elders.

I had been elected to the board a few months earlier and would now be a part of the decision-making process in the church. You will remember that I had made the observation years ago that most evangelical churches have on their boards men who are self-employed, successful, and middle aged. This was certainly true of our board. All of us were self-employed, middle aged, and successful in business (one man was retired from business). We met with the pastors who would be using our building (the lead pastor of the church would never be involved in any of these meetings, nor would we ever meet him), and they had some concerns. Because they were so invested in technology, they had certain requirements for sound, video, and lighting that we just did not meet. They suggested that we start a campaign to raise the money to upgrade these items (it was pitched that it would benefit our ministry as well), and when it was upgraded, they would begin to meet. We discussed with them how this partnership might benefit us. Their reply was that we could see how they did church and translate those practices into our service. We visited their mother church to see how they did things. It was pretty impressive, and they had hundreds of people who were new believers or nonbelievers attending their services and were bursting at the seams.

Richard was as insistent as he could be on partnering with them, and the board somewhat reluctantly agreed. They had seen all those people at the mother church, and though they were definitely more conservative philosophically they were at this point willing to do anything within reason to try and put people in the seats. So we approached the congregation with the idea of raising thousands of dollars to upgrade our sound, video, and lighting (as well as a new stage) so that we could team with a church that was reaching out into the community. It was never stated, to my knowledge, that we would be competing with another church in our own building. To put it another way, why, even if we upgraded our facilities, would someone attend our service when you could go to an even hipper service the night before? My thought was that if the other church grew as fast as they thought they might, we might just merge with them in a year or so and become one church, though I did not share that thought with anyone on the board; it was much too premature.

It was easier than we thought to raise the money. The congregation responded generously, and we began to upgrade our facilities with the help of the other church that had much more experience in that area than anyone in our church. The ability to raise the money may have had something to do with the fact that Richard gave an impassioned, tearful message where he basically said this was our last hope. It would become common in the next few years for the pastor to become emotional to the point of crying during many of his messages. If the reason was that he was being moved by the text or had compassion on his audience, that would have one thing. But most of those who were paying attention felt that he was depressed and so hard on himself for not living up to his own expectations that he felt himself a failure, and his emotions were constantly on the surface. For a man who was so careful to exhibit self-control, this was a troubling sign.

There was another troubling sign that was developing in our relationship with the other church, which was just starting to meet in our building Saturday nights. They had said that they were going to bring about 140 people to begin this church plant, but when they had their first service only about 80 people showed up. They had been meeting on Sunday morning at their previous location, and it turned out that many of the people just could not make the jump to Saturday night. Many churches now have services on Saturday evening, but these services are usually not the only option available. While Saturday night might work for some, I do not know of any church that has its only service on Saturday night, so it is not hard to see that there might be problems for a church that was only going to meet then. Eventually we got all of the upgrades accomplished and were looking forward to working with the other church to learn how to become more relevant to our neighborhood. It was at this point, only three months into our partnership, that there began to be trouble, trouble with a capital T.

First, the church we were partnering with began to have financial problems. The mother church had rented out the convention center in the city for Easter and had started a church with those who had come forward to become Christians. This church met in one of the meeting rooms at the convention center, and the thought was that they would transition this group into the Saturday night meeting at our church and have a group of about three hundred. But it was costing them thousands of dollars to keep that group going, and it was proving to be a stretch. When it was finally brought up to the group that they would be moving shortly to another location to meet on Saturday night, the group balked; they had been meeting on Sunday morning and did not want to change the time they met. The pastors had not counted on this and came to us to see how we might be able to accommodate them. We talked among ourselves and said they could have the church any time on Sunday after 12:30 p.m. They thanked us, but they really wanted to use the church auditorium during the 11:00 a.m. hour. We did not use the auditorium during that hour

(our service was at 9.30 a.m.), but we did not think it possible to run two completely different churches at the same time in the same building. There were nursery issues, parking issues, congestion issues; it just did not seem that we could do that for them, nor was it ever part of our original agreement with them. They said they would have to discuss this with the senior pastor and get back to us.

They did get back to us, and we met with them one night to find out how this was going to be resolved. They sat on one side of the table, and we sat on the other side. It was obvious from the moment they walked in the door from their body language that something was up. They were tense, they looked downcast to me, and there was none of the normal chitchat that happens before these kinds of meetings. The conclusion that they had come to (actually the conclusion that the senior pastor had come to—the guys who were actually doing the ministry at the church were not involved in the decision) was that if they could not have the 11:00 a.m. time they were going to take their toys and go home. We were all stunned; they threw down and expected us to cave. After all, they were the hip, growing, relevant church and we were the old, conservative, dying church. All of our reasons for not giving them that time, which to us seemed very valid and in no way selfish or unreasonable, were not even brought up; it was their way or the highway.

Though this meant the end of our partnership and could cause us problems with the congregation who had so recently given us thousands of dollars based on the fact that we were going to partner with a successful, growing church, we had the moral high ground because we had done nothing wrong and had motives as pure as the wind-driven snow. They were the ones who were going back on their word, leaving us in the lurch so to speak, and had displayed an arrogance that was quite unseemly. Those pastors knew what they were doing was wrong; you could read it all over their faces, but the decision was not theirs to make, and that was it. It was disappointing to me that the senior pastor of the emergent church never had the decency to come and meet with us in person but left his underlings to do the dirty work. I wonder if this is not more the norm than not in large successful churches that have grown largely as a result of one man's vision, energy, and speaking ability. The evangelical world is filled with stories of ministers whose position and power led them astray. I don't know if this would qualify, but it left us with a bad taste in our mouths.

It was at this point that I believe that Richard checked out emotionally and would soon begin to think about looking for another church. He viewed this partnership as his last chance to do something to reinvigorate the church, and it had failed, though the fault could not be laid at his feet. We had to explain this to the church, and they understood that these things happened, so there was no backlash or blame; indeed, things just went back to the way they had been, though we did have a much better sound system. The chairman of the elder board had been out of work for about a year, his business having failed due to overseas competition, and he had finally found a job that was in another city, so he was gone. Another elder decided not to stand for another term, and all of a sudden I became the chairman. There was only one other elder at this time, besides the pastor, and he was not interested, so it was almost by default that I assumed that role.

The church bylaws mandated that the church have five elders, but what do you do when you cannot get those who are qualified to serve? We asked several men to serve but were turned down each time. This did not really bother me. I didn't really care what the bylaws said, but it did make the dynamic different. The lower the number of elders, the more each elder's personality, views, philosophy, and opinions mattered. It would turn out that Charles was very conservative and traditional in nature, and though he said he was in favor of trying new things, you could tell his heart was not in it. Charles was afraid of change because change might result in people leaving, and that was what he feared the most. He was constantly counting the attendance numbers, wondering why so and so was not at church, always pondering what would happen if we did this or changed that or restructured something. He worried constantly about what the congregation would think on any given subject.

On the other hand, he was genuinely compassionate, liberal with his money (of which he had plenty), and a good teacher. He found it difficult to express himself in meetings; he would become tongue tied and constantly wring his hands when he spoke, which indicated to me that the meetings (and his participation as an elder) were way too important to him and had assumed a much larger role in his life than they should have. How can I say something like that? As I have mentioned before, some Christians find too much of their happiness, identity, meaning, and purpose in what happens at church, whether it is going to every meeting, holding some office, or being in a leadership position. Charles would sometimes plan his vacations so that he would be back on Sunday so as not to miss church, an indication to me that he might be wrapped way too tight. He micromanaged the pastor, was big on numbers, knew the budget inside and out, and could recite every circumstance from the church's past from memory. If the phrase "knowledge brings power" is true, then he had all the power in the church.

# Part Two: Phillip

By this point in his life, Richard had been at the church for almost twenty years, sixteen of those as senior pastor. How does a pastor know when to leave a church? Most people would say you pray about it and see how God might answer that prayer (some would say it's time to leave when your check bounces or when the chairman of the board won't return your calls), but really, do we pray about getting out of the way of a tsunami if one is coming? Do we pray about whether we should exercise or whether we should eat healthy? Some things in life are obvious, and God made us with the ability to know certain things without asking Him. If you have been at a church for twenty years and have given it all that you have and would like an opportunity to minister somewhere else and there is no compelling reason to stay, then look for another church. You can pray that God would bless your search and open or close doors, but the decision to leave would at this point in his life seem to be rather obvious.

Not everyone can succeed or thrive or have the right gifts for every circumstance, and it would become clear that the church needed something that he could not give at that point in its history. Still, in Richard's mind, there might have been the haunting aspect that he had failed. For a man to fail, especially one who set extremely high standards for himself and who was a perfectionist, that failure could be emotionally devastating. If he had come to us (the elder board) and said, "Guys, you need another pastor, and I need another church," we would have had no problem and helped him in any way that we could, but he did not do this. Few pastors give notice, as it were; most of them conduct the search for a new ministry opportunity in secret and then announce to the church they will be leaving soon. Many pastors do this because they have heard stories of men who have come back from vacation and found their furniture on the lawn of the parsonage, a not-so-subtle way of saying, "We believe God has called you to another ministry." So Richard began a search that would occupy him for about six months, and we were none the wiser.

Meanwhile, the church sort of returned to the status quo. The structural changes were still in place, but we were not growing, and the pastor's messages had assumed a sort of desperate tone to them. One leader in the church called them "self-loathing." He frequently said in his sermons how he had failed in this or that, and though he had been an excellent Bible teacher, this new tone was not encouraging; indeed, it was downright depressing. I think he was coming to the realization that his time at the church was coming to an end, and he would be leaving with the church having not grown at all during his ministry. Another pastor might have put some of the blame on some of us in the church, but he was not built that way; he took the whole burden on himself, and it showed. My wife was convinced that he was becoming clinically depressed and that I should go have a talk with him. If you remember, I had pretty much given up trying to get close to him (something that I really regret; I certainly could have tried harder) but thought that this was not a bad idea. I also had an idea that he might be looking for another church and wanted to ask him if that was true.

I came by the office one afternoon, and after exchanging pleasantries for a few minutes, I just came out and asked him how he was doing. To this, he said, "I am fine. Why do you ask?" I knew he was going to say that he was fine. To admit to any weakness would have way out of character for him, but I graciously pointed out to him what many of us had noted in his sermons—the discouragement, his being so hard on himself, the lack of joy, the emotions right on the surface. He just looked at me and said, "Oh, really? I didn't mean for anything like that to come across." Right there I just gave up again. I should have grabbed his collar and said, "What on earth are you talking about?" He was so in denial about his own condition that again I just gave up and asked him if he was looking for a new church. I knew that I did not have what it would take to help him see what others and I saw so clearly in his demeanor and behavior. In answer to my question, he replied, "Yes, there is a church that I have been in talks with, and I will be going out there in two weeks to preach and candidate." I was not surprised and was relieved that it was at last out in the open. Richard was pretty confident and promised to keep me abreast of the situation (it turned out that he had been recommended to the church by the man who had taught the church renewal seminar). So that was it. He would be gone in a few months, and the church would have to find a new pastor, something it had not done for almost twenty years. This fact confirms what I have been saying about the church: though it had its faults and its problems and was filled with sinners like every other church, the fact that the man managed to stay as pastor for sixteen years says something about the church. Most pastors last less than five years in the ministry.

Richard did end up being called to that church, and he announced it to the congregation about a month or so later. It was a secret that was well kept; I think only Charles and I knew what was going on. After his announcement, Richard's wife came to me and asked if my wife and I could arrange a meeting with Charles. It turned out that she had some things to say to him now that she was leaving the church. I knew what was going to happen, and I was not looking forward to this but felt it needed to done anyway. She had felt that it was Charles who had thwarted her husband's ministry over the years and made it so that he could not be successful and she wanted to tell him that. I had been at the church for about eight years by this point and had not seen anything like that from Charles and by now had been on the board with him for some time, but if she wanted this meeting, then she was going to have it. I talked with Charles prior to the meeting and told him what I thought was going to happen. He agreed with me and was willing to let her have her say.

To say that she had her say was putting it mildly. She came at him with guns blazing, accusing him of making it so that her husband could not be successful, using language that would make a sailor blush, letting him have all the accumulated hurts and disappointments that she had experienced at the church those twenty years. I will say this: it was Charles's finest moment. He was gracious. He did not respond in kind. He knew that in some primal way she needed this, and though she might not be correct in her assumptions, he sensed that she needed this type of moment before she could leave the church.

Believe it or not, the meeting did end on a somewhat positive note. My wife and I interjected a few comments here and there, Charles clarified a few things (he was in no way a doormat for her ravings), and because God is good, the meeting ended with at least some tacit agreement that he could have done more to help Richard and was sorry if he had said or done anything wrong and asked for forgiveness on his part. Richard's wife, once the emotion had drained out of her, returned to some kind of normal, and she left before he did. The three of us who were left let out a collective sigh of relief, glad that it was over. My wife made the observation that she had to leave her friends and career, and move to a new place where she would have to start completely over. My wife felt that much of her emotion was due to all of this hitting her at once, a way to try and give her the benefit of the doubt.

Before we get to the last part of our story, the search for a new pastor and how that turned out, I feel a need to give just an update on our personal story. This book has been about my experience at various churches, but the year that Richard left was an eventful one for us. Just before the pastor began to look for another church, my wife developed Guillain-Barre Syndrome. She was completely paralyzed for a time, missed six months of work, and though she would eventually recover almost completely, there were some residual effects. Then, about a year later, we both lost our jobs within a month of each other. The industry that I worked for had been going downhill for a number of years, so I was not that surprised, but the company where my wife was a vice president was in good shape; they were just trying to stay ahead of the curve, and they let go about a third of their officers. It took my wife nearly a year to find another job, one that paid about half of what she had been making. We lost our home and ended up living in a two-bedroom apartment, yet we'd never been happier. God provided for us that whole time and taught us many lessons that we would never have learned without that experience.

So back to our story. Richard served out his last two months (he would sell his home right before the housing bubble burst, lucky him), and then he was gone. When he left, there were only two elders on the board (Charles and me), so my first action was to add three new guys to the board to help in the search for a new pastor (the elder board was the search committee, though we sought the advice and counsel of others in the congregation). I had to practically beg two of the guys to serve on the board; both of them had been elders before and had not really liked how the board functioned. One of the guys, Frank, a retired man who had been at the church for decades, specifically told me that he would only serve a year. He said that he did not work well on boards, but if I wanted him to serve, he would. It would turn out that I should have listened to him.

I told them that things were different now and that I needed their wisdom, experience, and judgment in looking for a new pastor. The board would now be composed of me; Charles (he who bore the brunt of the pastor's wife's wrath); Simon, another self-employed businessman who was very successful and very smart; Jon, a man who worked for a software company who was involved in the music ministry of the church; and Frank, who at that time was my best friend at the church. We met for the first time at a restaurant on a Saturday morning, and the first thing we needed to do was to select a chairman. Because we would be without a pastor in a month, the position would have a little more responsibility than before. After some discussion, it became obvious that I would continue as chairman. I was now working for an organization that trained pastors (some irony there!) and was writing some of the material used in that ministry and had the flexibility to be at the church and oversee some of the things that the pastor did. I would do about a third of the preaching; two of the other elders were also able to help out, and we added a younger man in the church to the rotation, as well.

So the teaching was covered, and it would turn out that the church would appreciate the rotation we put together. I also suggested that we, for the time being, end our adult class and go to just a morning service, with a break in the middle for some refreshments and fellowship. The reason for this was that I did not think we could do the preaching and the teaching of a class at the same time and thought that a simpler church model while we looked for a pastor might be helpful and give some of our children's and nursery workers a much-needed break. Also, we did not know how a new pastor might want to structure the church, and the less we had, the less we might have to change. This idea was met with some resistance by the guys on the board; we thrashed it around for a few meetings, asked for the opinions of others in the church, and finally decided to give it a try.

The new format worked, especially the break after the worship time for refreshments and fellowship. From a teaching point of view, I thought it worked well to have people come back to their seats after about twenty or so minutes of visiting then listen to a message. People were awake, you could have some fun getting them back to their seats if you were the teacher, and it was a good experience for those on the board who did not think it would work to be proven wrong. This sounds harsh, but in life sometimes we need to be proved wrong in our opinions to be open to new things.

The first thing we did as elders was to meet with our denominational leaders to see how they might suggest we look for a new pastor. It turned out that their main concern was to help us get an interim pastor. I told them that we had the teaching covered and that I was in the office most days, and we had a secretary as well, so thanks but no thanks. They did not come out and say it, but they inferred that an interim would be able to do things that we could not and have experience that we did not have (I did not mention to them that I had been teaching and counseling pastors for years). It finally dawned on me that they had friends who were retired whom they wanted to get into churches as interim pastors so they could make some money; that was their main agenda in meeting with us. When it became clear that we were not going to go that route, they dropped it, no doubt thinking that we had made a huge mistake and would fall flat on our faces and come crawling back to them in a month or so. They did offer to send us the resumes of men who were looking for churches, and the meeting with them ended. We have not talked to them since, nor did they ever call us to see how we were doing.

Before we began the search for a pastor, at our first meeting at the restaurant, I did suggest that we might want to consider having an elder-run church, without a senior pastor, but I was almost laughed out of the room. It would have been a different model, I do not know if it would have "worked," but I like to think out of the box when it is appropriate. It took us about three months to get ready to begin the search for an actual candidate, and then we were off.

We did our search like nearly every other church: we looked at the resumes of men who were looking for new places to minister. As mentioned before, this method is fraught with danger, but what else were we going to do? We did not have an assistant we could promote; none of us knew of anyone who was looking for a church, so that left us with the resume route. One of the reasons why this method is potentially dangerous is that most of the men who are looking for a new church are looking to get out of another church. According to surveys of pastors, the main reasons why pastors leave churches is that they cannot get the church to accept their vision. Translated, this means that they cannot get either the board or the church to do what they want, so they get frustrated and leave, thinking they can find another church that will be more accommodating. One of things that quickly became apparent to us was that hiring someone who had been an assistant pastor would avoid some of the problems inherent in bringing on a man who had been a senior pastor. Yet an assistant might not have developed the skills that we were looking for. In our meetings, we looked over resumes trying to find those that we could agree on, men who in some measure fit the pastoral profile we had developed. It was not easy.

I need to say a word about our meetings. To put it mildly, there was some personality clash on our board. Two of the men in particular rubbed each other the wrong way and said things to each other that were insensitive, harsh, and in some cases cruel. The two men who clashed were Simon (the self-made businessman) and Frank (the retired man). In temperament, education, career, and outlook, the two men could not have been more different. Simon had always been the smartest guy in whatever room he happened to be in, and he did not suffer fools gladly. Which is a way of saying that if someone said something that he did not agree with, he just said so. He did not mean to be arrogant or annoying, but it came across that way. Frank had been a blue-collar worker all of his life, had only attended this church, and was for all practical purposes stuck in the 1960s. I had wanted him to be an elder (he had been one in the past) because he represented a certain segment of the congregation and was a godly man. We knew each other well and had done some traveling together, but his time on the board would test our friendship.

Although Frank had agreed with the rest of the board that we needed someone along the lines of a church planter, he really wanted more of a traditional pastor, a man who would focus mainly on teaching, visiting, and not shake things up too much. The board would eventually line up with three of us as more progressive and two as more conservative in terms of outlook, philosophy, and vision. Frank would make remarks about how rich Simon was and accuse me of listening more to him than the rest of the board (He did not know it, but the other elder, Charles, was pretty well off, as well). Three of us (Simon, Jon, and me) were on one side of the spectrum while Charles and Frank were on the more conservative side. It would seldom occur that we would have a meeting without some words being spoken that people would regret later (at least I hope they regretted them).

Frank and Simon just could not speak to each other without insulting or criticizing the other. Simon would constantly be annoyed that Frank could not grasp a particular point, at which point Frank would make some kind of obnoxious remark, and on it would go. I could have stopped it as chairman, and perhaps I should have, but I felt the group needed to find its own dynamic and find ways to disagree yet still trust and work with each other. It drove Charles completely nuts that I would not interrupt these two when they got going, so he took it upon himself to defend Frank, who was the one who usually lost his composure. Simon never lost his composure, which made matters worse in some respects. It would turn out that I now believe I made a mistake by asking Frank to be an elder. He was not suited emotionally or by temperament to be an elder; at least that is what I came to think. We did get our business done, but not without some strained relationships, but more on that later.

We started with forty resumes, and we circulated these among the five of us to find a consensus of who we should begin to look at first.

We decided to start with five men on whom we could all agree and proceed from there. It took a while, but we did find five men who in some way fit into the general parameters of the pastoral profile. These guys were all over the map in terms of experience, age, education, and location. The first guy that struck us all was a man who was leaving the army as a chaplain; he had been in about six years and wanted to work in a church again. He was about thirty-five, had two kids, and seemed very evangelistic and outgoing from what we could glean. We contacted him and talked to him by phone and asked him a number of questions that we hoped might give us an indication of who he was and what he was like. You can only do so much on the phone, but it was all positive. It turned out that he was going to be in our part of the country in two weeks speaking at another church; he would be glad to come and talk to us in person if we would like.

We agreed to this, and someone asked if he would like to preach that Sunday, not as a candidate, just to fill the pulpit and let us see how he was as a speaker. In retrospect, this was not a good idea, but he said yes, he would like to do that (when you have someone come and speak at your church when you are looking for a pastor, there is no way some people will not view him as a candidate. After he spoke, some people came up to me and said he would make a good pastor). His name was Stanley, and we met with him two weeks later for dinner at one of the elder's homes. We had all put him number one of the five that we had all agreed upon and entered the meeting with him thinking that perhaps this would be a short search. No such luck. We settled around a table and began to talk with him, asking him specifically how he would grow a church. He hemmed and hawed for a while, talking in generalities, but it turned out he had no idea how to grow a church, no plan, no process, no vision, and no experience. He was probably someone who could be very evangelistic personally, but that is not the same as growing a church. His fate was sealed, at least in my mind, when we asked him if he had any questions for us.

He said no, he didn't. There was no way he could have learned enough about the history of the church, our circumstances, the former pastor, and what we believed as elders from our time with him. That he was not in the least bit curious to ask us any questions, or perhaps that he did not know enough to ask any questions, that settled the issue for me. It did not, however, settle the issue for some of the other guys. They liked him as a person, thought he could work, and believed that he might bring some needed energy to the church. When I pointed out my concerns and the fact that there was no way I was going to recommend him, that put an end to the discussion. We had agreed that we would only move forward with someone if we all agreed, so that was the end for Stanley. It will not perhaps come as a surprise to you that the two conservative guys on the board, Frank and Charles, were more disposed toward Stanley than the rest of us; he would have been a safe choice and much more in the role of a traditional pastor.

We had gone through two of our five people and were not discouraged, but we realized we might be in for a long haul. We were determined to find the right person, so we did not mind a long search. Things were going well at the church; we had actually gained a few people in the interim, so there was no pressure. The only real pressure was whether Frank and Simon could make it together on the board and not come to blows (a slight exaggeration, but not much).

The next guy we talked to was also close to the city, so we had him come in the next week. He was the pastor of a church that had gone through some difficulty, and he basically wanted out. He had stayed at the church through those problems, helped get the people through that difficult time, and felt they would be better off with someone else. He had taken the position of senior pastor after the previous man had left, done a good job, but now wanted to find a new position (my guess was that not all of the problems had been resolved; sometimes in interviews people reveal things that they do not realize or intend to reveal). I admired him for his honesty, but he seemed really beaten down to us, and he also did not know how to grow a church, nor had he ever done it before. It would turn out that what the men we interviewed really felt called to do was preach.

When they did give an answer to the question of how you grow a church, it was always along the lines of, "Preach and teach the Word." Three down, two more to go until we exhausted the first group and started over.

The next man was an associate pastor in California, a young man who seemed to us to have the requisite experience and vision that we were looking for. He had helped grow the college group at his church, he had worked at a church plant with another man for a time, and he listed in his resume a number of statements that indicated to us that he might have the energy, personality, and talents to help us renew the church. We knew that he had not been a senior pastor, with the attendant responsibility, but we felt he would be worth talking to on the phone to see how he might respond to our questions. I don't know why we didn't Skype with these men instead of doing phone calls. Skype is a free video-conference program that is now used by millions of people (our family uses it nearly every day to keep in touch with each other). It shows you how fast technology changes that just two years later we would have been able to see the people that we were talking to on the phone. I was prepared to like this guy, and when we talked to him, I was not disappointed. He talked about his experience working with young people, how he had worked in a church plant for about a year, how they got that church up and running, and he talked about his young family.

I thought this kid could work for us; it would be nice to have as the face of the church a young man with young kids. We asked him how he might work with a board where the members were much older than he was. He did not think that would be a problem and had an air of confidence that I found reassuring. Then he said something that brought the conversation to an uncomfortable pause. He knew that we would talk to his references, and he knew that it would come out that about seven years previously he had a problem with viewing pornography on the Internet. I asked him to give us a brief history of this problem, and he shared with us he just fell into temptation; it was something that he believed happened to him because he was at a low point spiritually in his life at that time. It never developed into anything physical and only lasted a few months. He was not caught; he came to his senses, as it were, and went to his pastor, who helped him with a plan to keep from falling back into the same pattern again. He did not leave his position with the church, the pastor and the young man told the elders about what had happened, and he had not had a problem since that time.

Because he knew that we would find out about this because the pastor who had helped him was one of his references, I wondered if he would have told us if no one else had ever found out. He was being honest with us, but then he had to be; he really had no choice. I took the lead in the conversation, and after talking about this for a few minutes, I told him we would have to discuss this among ourselves and get back to him. I told him that for me this was not something that would remove him from being considered but that I could not speak for the group (I got a few glances from the group for giving my opinion out in the open before we discussed the matter). I knew that when we discussed this there were going to be sparks; it was pretty easy to read the body language of the guys. We ended the conversation, telling the young man that we would get back to him within a day or so, and then we began to discuss this revelation.

I love the Internet, and I hate the Internet. I love that I can do much of my ministry electronically, I can send files around the world, I can videoconference with people on several continents simultaneously, I can research, I can shop, I can book travel, and I can order food for goodness' sake. I hate the Internet because it is so easy to use it to sin, especially in terms of sexually explicit material. Men and women who might never have fallen into sexual sin have succumbed to the temptation that websites on the Internet offer. It would turn out that this young man would not be the only candidate we talked to who had problems in this area, but he was the only one whom we really thought could become the pastor of our church. I did not have a problem with his past indiscretion, if indeed he had been "clean" for the last seven years. Because he had given it up himself, had confessed to his pastor when he did not have to (no one would have ever known; one of the allures of the Internet is its supposed anonymity), been in an accountable relationship to a man who knew of this past sin, and had his wife monitor his Internet usage, I felt that this should not disqualify him from consideration. Most of the guys felt the same way, though with reservations.

Frank just could not get past the fact that we would consider someone who had viewed pictures of naked women. He thought that we were being much too lenient and almost permissive; this type of sin was much worse than other sins and revealed a measure of depravity in someone who would do such a thing. I agreed with him but pointed out that sexual sin was listed in groups of other sins that were just as bad. It is interesting to note that in two lists of sins that Paul writes about, sexual sin is equated with greed and slander; see 1 Corinthians 6:9-10 and Ephesians 5:3. How many churches have men on their boards that have made their fortunes because they are greedy, yet churches many times will view these men as having been "blessed" by God and their success as an indication that they are qualified to lead in the church? I pointed out that this was a common problem among pastors; at least we knew in this case what we were getting. Statistics compiled by groups that surveyed pastors have found that up to thirty percent of pastors have viewed pornography on the Internet. If we ended up talking to ten candidates, the odds were that at least one or more of them might have done the same thing as this young man (it was never brought up in our group if any one of us had this particular problem). The four of us did not consider that this problem should cause the man to be disqualified, but we could not persuade Frank.

I think that because he came from a different generation, sex was just harder for him to talk about, let alone sexual sin. I had sat in churches for decades and had never heard a sermon on sexual sin, let alone on how to overcome it. Because of that, I had taught a series a few years earlier in my adult class on "Everything the Bible Says about Sex," not realizing at the time how much the Bible does actually talk about sex, particularly sexual sin. Frank did not want to keep us from considering the guy if he was the only one who found this a disqualification, so he agreed that it was worth having the young man come to visit us and talk with him face-to-face. This made Frank a minority of one, and in his mind, he would come to feel that he was standing up for traditional morality and doctrinal purity, a lone voice on the elder board for all things biblical, but most of that would be in the future. We called the young man back the next day and asked him if he could fly up and talk to us. He agreed, but it would have to wait for a week or so; he had some commitments that he could not avoid. That was fine with us; we had one more person to talk to on our list, and we would see him then.

You can see why churches can get discouraged in looking for a new pastor or why they will sometimes hire someone they shouldn't. This would not be the last time that I would think this was an idiotic way to find someone to lead a church. Why the church could not raise up and train their own leaders still remains a mystery to me; traditional evangelical churches are so wedded to the Bible college/ seminary pattern that I fear it may never be broken. But we had to use what we had, and this was the only real option open to us, so we anticipated talking with the guy from California and seeing where that would take us.

God, however, had other plans. Our church worship leader, a woman who was a graduate of the local seminary, knew a man from college who had been a pastor for over fifteen years and who was now out of the ministry and working in the business world. He had worked in three churches; two he had resurrected, as it were, and the last one he had worked in was a church plant. She had spoken to him and asked if he might be interested in our position. It would turn out that she had e-mailed him a month earlier to an account that he seldom looked at, so he did not express interest until we were well along in the process.

He sent his resume to us the day after we had talked to the two men and had made arrangements to bring the one guy up to talk to us, so he was coming in late in the process. I was at the church the day his resume arrived, so I printed it out and looked it over. My first thought was, *Why is this guy interested in us?* He was obviously overqualified; he should have been looking for a larger church, one that was not on its last legs, so to speak. He had been to seminary and had supplemented his education by attending a number of church growth and church management seminars, as well as speaking at those same types of events. He had demonstrated the ability to turn around and grow churches. The question I needed answered was why he was now in the business world and out of the ministry? I sent the resume out to the other elders. They were definitely interested, and so I called him and set up a phone conference for that night.

We had been meeting weekly (and sometimes more) for the last several months, and the toll this was taking on us was beginning to tell. We had this enormous decision before us, and the process was only in the beginning stages. All of the elders had other responsibilities and had been giving much time and energy to this search for the right man. There was tension on the board that just would not go away. I had to talk to three of the guys individually and ask them to dial down their emotions and words. They were all good, decent men, but the combination of circumstances and personality was having its effect on the group. If just one of the two men, Simon or Frank, had not been on the board, we would have functioned seamlessly and without all of the drama. I am pretty sure that we would have come up with the same outcome if one of them had not been on the board, but hindsight is always perfect. I am continually amazed by the things that supposedly mature Christians will say at times, comments that are critical, hurtful, and personal to the extreme. And then we close the meetings with prayer? After some of our meetings, I just couldn't say anything other than, "We're done. Let's go home. It's late." Sometimes I would just close by praying something like, *Lord, You know we do love each other; help us to act like it next time.* It has been pointed out by innumerable people that the phrase "Sticks and stones can hurt my bones, but words can never hurt me" is completely false. I know that some of the things said in the room changed the way some of the elders would feel and relate to each other in the future. Words can destroy relationships over time. We would survive as a group but barely and not without some lasting effects.

So we met the next evening to talk with the next guy (his name was Phillip). We had all looked at the resume, and each one of us realized that he was the most experienced and qualified candidate that we had yet come across, but we wanted to know why he was all of a sudden looking to get back into the ministry. It would turn out that he had not been looking for a church when he found out about us but was contemplating returning to the pastorate. After exchanging pleasantries, we first asked him about why he left the ministry. Phillip explained that at his last church, which he had started as a church plant and had grown to 320 in about four years, he had become burned out by the workload and needed a break. He was the oldest and most mature person in the church (what he meant was that nearly everyone at the church was young and a new believer), and he had to shoulder nearly all of the decision making, teaching, counseling, etc.

Three days later we were sitting together in the basement room of an elder's home for our first meeting with the man who would become our pastor. The first thing Phillip did was to ask us individually about our families, our jobs, our backgrounds, our church experience, and what we thought the church needed right then. No one else whom we talked to approached us in this manner, so he set himself apart from everyone else right from the start. It became apparent as we talked that he knew the "business" of church—how a board should function, how a church should be structured, and how a church should grow. He also was not shy about saying that there would probably need to be many things that would have to be changed and that if he came he would want that understood from the start. When asked what things, he said things like the church documents; he had read them, and they were not relevant to a church this size anymore. They were written when the church was 450 people; they would need to be changed to fit the church in this time. He also said he did not think the church needed a secretary; most churches had changed this position to one of administrative assistant. He would want control over the staff and have authority on whom to hire and whom to fire, though he would run that by the elders. He was very matter of fact about these things. There was no arrogance or control; that was what he needed to be successful, and he wanted to be up front about everything.

Since I had lost my job in the "secular" world, I had been spending a lot of time at the church, writing curriculum for the organization I was working for as a church consultant, working with the worship director and youth pastor, and had observed a few things about the secretary. First, the phone hardly ever rang, maybe three or four times a day. True, we did not have a pastor at the time, but I could see from the caller ID that most of the calls were either sales calls or older people calling to find out what was going on at the church. She worked from 8:00 a.m. to 12:00 p.m. (she had cut back to part time a few years earlier when she was eligible for Social Security), and it began to dawn on me that she really didn't do anything to speak of. We were not paying her very much, but still. Every time she did do something, she was sure that I knew it; it was like she was justifying her job on a daily basis. She had no computer skills to speak of, was not really able to help the other staff with anything, so when the candidate mentioned that she would have to go, I had no problem. I had been pointing out to the guys that she really didn't do much of anything, and two of the elders wanted her gone, but the other two were pretty adamant that she was a presence at the church, had been there for years, and we could afford her, so what was the big deal about keeping her? Can you guess who wanted to keep her? If you said the two conservative elders, please go to the head of the class. So if we hired this guy, one of the first things that we would have to do was fire the church secretary, and by *we* I mean the elders. He did not think it appropriate for his first act to be letting someone go who had worked at the church for years, so we would have to do that. He said that if she wasn't let go, it would become obvious that she could not do the things that he would require, and the situation would only become worse as time went on.

We knew instinctively that he was right, but Charles and Frank tried to find some scenario under which she could stay. I will say this for Phillip: he knew what he wanted, he knew what he needed to be successful, and he did not budge, though he did it with grace. He told us that many more things were going to change if the church was going to survive; we might as well get used to it. You had to admire his approach. Most guys would not come into an interview telling you they were going to change everything in your church, but he was not like the other guys we interviewed. Phillip knew that a church like ours would need to be overhauled to become renewed and did not want any misunderstandings, miscommunications, or anyone saying to him, "You never said that!" It would emerge that he was a good leader and knew how to get most people on board for nearly all of what he wanted to do.

This is not to say that he was perfect. He admitted to us that he was not very organized, not much of a detail person, tended to move ahead on his own more often than not, and that this had gotten him into trouble before. He said this to us so we could help him with these weaknesses and help hold him accountable for the things he set out to do. As we talked, it became obvious that we were going to seriously consider him, so we asked him about his availability. Here we hit a snag. He would have to sell his home and give notice at his job. He wanted to come part time for six months and then transition to full time. He said that this would be better for the church. He would be so different from Richard that if he came full time from the start, it would be something of a shock (in this he would prove to be correct; even half time was something of a shock for many people). We asked him if his family was okay with the suddenness of his decision to get back into the ministry, specifically about coming to this church. It turned out that his wife's parents lived only about thirty miles away, his son was attending college in our town, and his brother lived just south of the city, so while it would be a disruption of their lives, there were some obvious pluses.

We met without him the next day while he was still in town to discuss what we wanted to do. Four of us were all for moving ahead and bringing him before the church as a candidate (we would need to call his references and verify some details). My guess is that you know who was in the minority. He had never run across a pastor who pretty much said what he thought, knew what he wanted to do, wanted to change everything in the church, and was pretty up front about it all. We knew that we would not find anyone as qualified or more qualified, and some of us appreciated his candor and honesty. Again, the retired elder reluctantly gave his approval, again making himself a minority of one.

Churches have a tendency to hold pastors to ridiculously high standards, standards that they do not hold for themselves. It is true that there are standards and requirements listed in the New Testament for leaders in the church, but you can find nearly every one of those qualities listed someplace else as a normal behavior or characteristic for "ordinary" believers. Things like temperance, hospitality, not quarrelsome, not a lover of money, not violent, gentle, a good reputation with those who are not Christians—all of these should be true of every believer and are listed in different places in the New Testament as traits that should be true of all Christians. Because churches have perhaps an unrealistic view of pastoral spirituality, they are much harder on them when they show themselves to be human and sin or make bad choices just like everyone else. Pastors contribute to this mentality by not admitting to weakness, living double or secret lives, and seldom have anyone that they can confide in or help them when they are tempted or weak.

So now we had to figure out how to bring him before the church. We had him come for two weekends to meet with as many people as he could and to preach to the congregation. Because he was so outgoing and sincerely liked people, he did not have any problem relating to most of the people in the church. There were a few that thought he was too forward, but that was just who he was. He liked to press the flesh, and it showed. He had also told us that he would naturally gravitate toward the unbelievers in a group, and that might upset some who thought he might be slighting them. As elders, we thought this was great; that was what we were looking for in a pastor.

He brought his family out those two weekends, and both his wife and daughter seemed to be okay with all of the attention they were getting; they had after all been through this before. They would be the ones that would have the harder adjustment. Their whole life was in this other state, and they would have to pick up and start over again. Plus, she would be giving up a job that she loved; she worked with at-risk kids in her local school district. It was as much a ministry as a job. In addition, they would be taking a substantial (about half) cut in pay if he accepted the position. After being in the ministry for over fifteen years then having a job that paid really well, that would be a real adjustment in living standard for them as a family. They had been able to do things that they could never have done on a pastor's salary (like take a vacation or have a nice house and a horse); all that would be gone. He knew that he was not called to be a businessman, but like he assured us, he was human, and he would miss some of the things that money could provide. It was a measure of his character that he was willing to throw all of that away and go back into the world of being a pastor on a modest salary, knowing that as a pastor he was never going to have the resources he had when he worked in the business world (like help his kids through college).

We had a church business meeting where we brought Phillip up for a vote, and I went through the history of how we as a board had arrived at the point where we were recommending that we vote him in as our pastor. After all of the work we had done and all of the emotion that we expended on getting to that point, somewhere in my remarks I just lost it and turned away and began to weep. One of the other elders took over for me, and we proceeded to the vote. The man and his family were in a classroom praying together. I think that they knew we were going to call him/them, but they made a decision that if he did not get at least 90 percent in favor of him coming, they would decline. He did not need to worry; only one person voted against calling him, though I suspect if the vote had been taken a year later, he would not have received anywhere near that high a percentage.

So now we had a pastor, but only part time. He would fly out for a week then go back to his hometown. He had a pretty flexible job. In that he was lucky. He could do some of it from his office at the church, and he would not give notice for another five months, one month before he began full time at the church. He was right about it being best that he only come part time at the start; he was the Energizer Bunny incarnate. He had told us that he did not keep office hours; he preferred to meet with people during the afternoon and evening hours, so he did not begin work until after noon. He spent those first few months visiting everyone in the church and found out things about people that we as elders never knew; he had a way of getting past the routine small talk to personal issues and history so that he could understand the person he was talking with. He also had us give the church secretary notice, and by *us* I mean me and Charles.

Charles dreaded the conversation that we would have with her, though he agreed to do it. I think that she might have known what was coming, but she pretended to be surprised when we talked with her. We told her that we were doing away with the position, not doing away with her. We thanked her for her years of service, tears were shed, and that was that. This caused no small disturbance in the church, especially among the older folks. We could not come out and say that she basically did not do anything and had become irrelevant, that she did not possess the skills needed to be an administrative assistant to the pastor; we did not want to demean her in that way.

She would leave the church within two weeks, giving up on all of the relationships that she had built over the years, throwing it all away because she probably thought people would think she was fired when that was not the case at all. She was over retirement age, could have easily told people she was retiring (which she did), and stayed at the church. But pride can be a terrible thing—that and the ability to misjudge people's motives. She took the action much too personally, which you can understand, but then could not come back from the brink and get over it. I suspect there was some subtle embarrassment in knowing that at least I was aware that she really did not do anything, but that was never mentioned to her; indeed, we went out of our way to handle the situation with as much tact and grace as we could. We paid her for two months and bought her a new computer (a little irony there), but she was gone, and some people just never got over it, though no one left over that incident.

Phillip had told people that there were going to be changes, but many were taken aback when change actually happened. He had other new things in mind and laid them out for us when we had an elders' retreat soon after he began working full time. Most seminaries teach their students that when they assume their first pastorate, they are not to make any substantial changes for at least a year. They need that first year to get to know people, to build up goodwill; they need to focus on teaching and preaching. But then, as I have mentioned before, most seminaries do not teach what church is really like or how to bring about meaningful and lasting change. His view was that our church had perhaps one chance to become renewed, and there was no sense in waiting around to begin the process. Might as well get all the pain over at once and do as much as we could as fast as we could, keeping the congregation informed but proceeding ahead apace.

One of the first things Phillip had noticed was that the church looked like a holdover from the 1970s, with hideous green carpet and a lobby that said, "Welcome to your grandfather's church." He had someone he knew in interior design come in and for free give us some ideas on how to remake the interior of the church so that it was more inviting and more coordinated. He wanted to enlarge the lobby, build a small visitor's center, and have a corner in the lobby to serve coffee (many people stopped at Starbucks on their way to church and brought their coffee with them). His idea was that if you wanted to reach people in the community, you needed to make the church a place that gave off a good first impression. When we finished the lobby, it did end up looking much like a Starbucks, and nearly everyone commented on the improvement in the look of the church.

The auditorium took longer to finish, but it, too, was a great improvement over what we had previously. We added blinds to control the lighting, got rid of the hideous green carpet, made the auditorium smaller to feel more intimate, and updated the sound booth. All of this cost money, so we went to the congregation when we had developed a plan for everything and asked people to give. It should be mentioned that our church had a number of wealthy individuals, and the money was raised and spent over a period of about nine months. People were generous. We held numerous meetings to communicate (as opposed to getting people's opinions—we did not solicit any advice from the congregation on what color of carpet they liked, what kind of lighting fixtures were good, etc.) what we were doing and how we were progressing. Phillip was the man in charge, and though he kept the elders informed of what was going on, we all knew it was his project. He had specifically asked for this kind of authority while he was a candidate, and we granted it because he had the experience and we did not. But to know something in your head and then to experience it firsthand, well, it was hard for a couple of the guys, and you know who I mean.

Frank had agreed to serve for a one-year term, and his year was just about up. As previously noted, he had a rocky year on the board. He continually found himself alone in his opinions and clashed with Simon and occasionally Jon. He was not temperamentally suited to be an elder. He just could not function in meetings, he said things that did not reflect who he really was, and he needed to go off the board. Both Phillip and I knew this and would have to talk to him about not standing for another term when his was up. This would turn out to be one of the hardest things I had ever done, and our relationship would not be the same, though we would remain friends.

When I had asked Frank to come on the board, he had agreed to come on reluctantly and then only for a year. I think that he knew he was not suited to be an elder (though he had been one in the past) and that it might bring out the darker part of his nature. He now wanted to stay on the board because he felt that we needed his perspective (again, I am convinced he felt he was standing alone as the guardian of doctrine and morals on the board) and wanted to be involved in the decisions we were making. Yet it was obvious that he was going to be against most of those decisions, and for reasons that could be summarized in the phrase, "We have never done it that way before" or, "You (the pastor) have way to much power." He seemed to be opposed to change just because it was change, not for any reasons (either biblical or practical) that he could articulate. He knew the world was changing, that the church probably needed to change as well to become or stay relevant, but it was just not in him to be for anything new. Had his behavior in the board meetings been less volatile, had he been able to understand the reasons why we were doing the things we were (we constantly had to keep explaining over and over to him the reasons why we needed to redo the lobby, change the bylaws, etc), then we might have been able to keep him with us, but it was just not going to work. Phillip and I met with him after the service one Sunday and asked him politely not to stand for election at the upcoming business meeting, reminding him that he had agreed to serve just one term.

Unfortunately, he did not see it that way and was shocked that we would ask him not to serve and then to suggest that being an elder was not the best way for him to serve God. He was great at dealing with people one on one, carried on a consistent program of visiting many of the shut-ins, and ran a prayer group. We tried to explain that it had become obvious he did not enjoy being an elder, that he was constantly upset at the meetings, and that we were just trying to find the best place for him to serve. Frank thought we were trying to get him off the board so that the pastor could have even more control, and he threw it out that he might need to leave the church, for what reason I do not know (he did not leave the church and is still active in many different ministries). He basically said that he would be watching what we did to make sure that we did not go off the deep end doctrinally. I took a little offense at that, and the pastor had to bring the conversation back to our purpose. It did not end well; there was a lot of tension left in the room when he left. Phillip and I were glad that it did not go worse, but we were both drained. It was the hardest thing we had done up to that point, and we thought that there was an even chance that he would leave the church.

So we had handled two crises, the letting go of the secretary and asking Frank not to run for another term. These would be the two most difficult things we did in the first few months. We would proceed with the other changes. The only one that brought out some opposition was when we decided to rewrite the bylaws of the church. They were written when the church was much larger and had now grown obsolete. Besides the fact that they were outdated, we had not been able to get people to serve on these boards that were detailed in the bylaws; they were so ill defined that nobody wanted to commit themselves for a one- or three-year term. What we basically did was to consolidate all of the decision-making authority in the board of elders, who would function as the leaders of the church and oversee all of the church's ministries.

The pastor would be in charge of the staff, the staff would mobilize the congregation to do the actual work of ministry, and the elders would set policy and guard the doctrine and practice of the church. This meant that in this new structure the elders would not be involved in the day-to-day operations of the church, nor know everything that was going on; that responsibility was given to the pastor, who would manage the staff who, along with the members of the church, would do the work. This made sense to me and Jon, who did not want to micromanage the church; we were more than willing to let the pastor have that responsibility and carry it out through the staff and the laity.

However, Charles (we were now down to three elders and the pastor; Simon stepped down due to his many other commitments) had real problems with this type of elder board. Charles had been an elder for over twenty-five years and felt it was part of being an elder to know what was happening in every facet of the church. He loved to discuss any issue, ministry, person, or problem that we were having and give his opinion on how to deal with it (he frequently sent out e-mails on different things happening in the church—"Have we dealt with this? Do we realize that? What will happen if?"—you get the point). Charles did not like the fact that I was still the chairman after about four years; he felt that I was too laid-back in my leadership and did not pay enough attention to details. This was true, because I wanted Phillip to have the freedom to use his experience and gifts to get the church back on track, and I did not want to be the one setting the agenda for our meetings and what we would cover. I had always felt that the position of chairman, if practiced the way it had been practiced in the past, hindered the ministry of the pastor. Charles complained about me to the pastor and in meetings took up an inordinate amount of our time dealing with things that nobody else wanted to talk about. When my term as chairman was up, he went to the pastor to lobby for the position, again citing my shortcomings, but Jon and Phillip were all on the same page philosophically, so his efforts went nowhere. At the next meeting, I was elected chairman again, but the position was pretty much a formality, I think to the chagrin of Charles, who wanted the job. I do not want to suggest that he was a schemer or wanted control of the board; he just had a different view of how an elder at our church should function and had difficulty accepting the new order of things.

So life at church goes on. We are still in the midst of setting a foundation from which to start aggressively reaching out to the community. The pastor has been adamant that we cannot begin to think outwardly until we have the physical changes to the church finished and new ministries in place to work with those who will visit or come to the church. In the first year of the pastor having been here full time; we accomplished more change and put in place more new structures than anyone could have imagined, and though there have been rough spots on the journey, we have mostly held the church together through all of this, and I anticipate that we will experience a time of real growth in the near future, but only God knows that. My opinion is that many of the congregation never gave up the hope that God would again use the church in the community as in the past and that God will reward their patience, prayers, and hope with a renewed church that will find ways to be relevant and meaningful in the lives of those God brings to us.

## Principles for the Pastor

1. *Members with money.* Most churches have people who would be considered well off or even affluent. This is a fact that most pastors are no doubt aware of and that may have already influenced their ministry for either good or bad. When I was younger, I generally distrusted rich people. I mistakenly thought that to be rich you had to have done something morally questionable to attain wealth. With time I have come to realize that many people are wealthy through no fault of their own; their hard work, intelligence and perhaps luck regarding timing and circumstance have made it possible for them to accumulate lots of money. Of course, there are those who desire to get rich and have succeeded; churches have both types of wealthy people. The New Testament does not seem to condemn the first type of rich person (1 Tim. 6:17-19) but does have some harsh words for those who have become rich through an inordinate desire to obtain wealth (1 Tim. 6:9-10).

   Those with money can both help and hinder a church. They can help by using their resources to provide for the church when others cannot; they can also use their status as being rich to have power, control, or undue influence in the affairs of the church. Since there is usually no financial gain for those who are rich to be found in the church, it seems that the accumulation of power and influence are most often what rich people are after. There are, of course, rich people who try and remain either anonymous in the church or do not seek any specific position or influence and still gladly share what they have. Pastors may personally benefit from a rich person's generosity; many pastors have benefactors who will help supplement their salary with gifts of either money or services. I have seen pastors benefit greatly from having this type of person in their church, and I have also seen pastors defer to the wishes and opinions of their benefactor in terms of church policy, strategy, and vision. I am all for letting people who have means help pastors financially (most pastors are underpaid as it is), but this type of help can come with strings attached. Just because a pastor may take the help offered does not mean he has to let the strings guide what he does as the leader of the church. I would caution against accepting help from those who may have obtained their wealth through greed or an unhealthy desire for power (if their motives can be discerned); this will cause trouble in the future. Those in the congregation usually know those who are rich. If they see that the rich have undue influence over the pastor or that he is too solicitous toward them, it will harm his integrity.

2. *Thoughts on sermons.* Pastors spend a lot of time and energy preparing and preaching sermons. For many of them this practice is why they wanted to become a pastor. Here are some random thoughts on this subject.

   a. **A Pastor's sermons set the tone for the church.** Because the worship service is usually the only time the church meets together, and the sermon takes around half of that service, what the pastor says is viewed as what the church is about, for good or bad. A pastor can promote hope, encouragement, grace, acceptance, compassion, holiness, and love by how and what he preaches. Similarly, he you can promote legalism (the more you do, the more God loves you), intolerance (we are better than those who are not Christians), separatism (we are better than those who do not believe like us), and indifference (lack of compassion for those whose who are different) by what he says and how he says it.

b. **A Pastor's sermons are not going to change the lives of those who hear them.** I have already touched on this previously, but it is worth repeating. Messages can set the tone for the church, provide information on the Bible, provide the congregation with the vision the pastor has for the church, and deal with specific behaviors, values, and issues. But they will not alone mature people into the image of Christ. Discipleship happens in the context of relationship; look up all the passages in the New Testament that contain the phrase "one another." Those pastors who believe that their sermons are the most important thing for their members to experience are saying in essence that all they have to do is attend Sunday morning and listen to him preach.

c. **Preaching is not performing.** There is a fine line between being a good communicator and putting on a show. Pastors can learn how to be better speakers, pastors can learn how to use illustrations and video in their messages, but they cannot learn from a class or book how to become more passionate or sympathetic to those they see before them when they preach. These things are learned from time spent in prayer for the congregation; a man knows his prayers have been answered when he is not concerned about how he spoke but what God did through his words.

3. *Talking about Jesus in church.* A pastor has just finished the morning service. The church has sung songs in which they worshipped Jesus, they have prayed to Jesus, the pastor has delivered a message in which Jesus may have figured prominently, and now he is in the lobby visiting with his people. Why isn't anyone talking about Jesus? People will talk to him about his sermon, they will talk about sports, they will ask about his family, they will want to know things about the church, but they seldom talk about the One they just spent an hour or so supposedly worshipping! You might think I am being overly critical, but this has bothered me for decades (as you can tell). I don't know why this is exactly, though I have some thoughts. My bigger concern is how the pastor might be able to help people in the church talk to each other about their Savior. Evangelicals use the phrase "personal relationship with Jesus," but I do not see much evidence of that relationship at church functions. Here are some ideas that a pastor might consider to break this pattern that exists in most churches.

   a. In your sermons, reference your own experience and relationship with Christ.

   b. In your board meetings, ask your leaders not only about their spiritual lives but their relationships with Christ. Paul was not shy about telling others what Christ meant to him and how Christ was the source of his strength and life.

   c. If you have small groups, you might be able to find material that would help your members become more open about their relationships with Christ. You can certainly train your small-group leaders develop a process (through questions, testimonies, encouragement) to begin talking about how their members experience the life of Christ in their own spirits.

d.  In your conversations during church meetings, rise above the ordinary. Do not worry about appearing more spiritual than your members; don't worry about how you will come across. Just find ways that are natural to bring Jesus into the conversations you have with your congregation.

e.  Finally, it is good to remember that the reason that many of your people do not talk about Jesus is that they have nothing to talk about. People can attend church for years and not have developed a relationship with Christ that is real, dynamic, and experiential. Your example, words, and messages can help them discover who they have been missing.

4.  *Leading Through Change: Part One.* Once your church has agreed to make certain changes, whatever they might be, it will be your responsibility to lead this change and see that it is accomplished. I am going to assume that you have developed a plan, communicated this to your board and gotten their approval, held meetings with your church to go over the need for change, the plan for change, and how the change will benefit the church and help meet the needs of the congregation. Your board and church can all be agreed that changes need to be made and agree on how to do it, but when things get rolling, some in your church will still have difficulty and will question again the need for change, the process to bring about the change, etc.

It is one thing to know and to agree to something intellectually; it is another thing entirely to experience that change on a continual basis. You must expect this type of behavior, but you must also be adamant that this is what you as a church all agreed on and not allow the objections of some to derail your process. One church I attended tried to change the nature of how people became members, proposing the idea of covenant membership, which as a consequence would have meant purging many people from the membership rolls: people who had left the church, people who seldom attended the church, and those who were in nursing homes. Some board members got incensed at the thought that those who were once a part of the church would have their names removed from the church roll, even though they might not have been in the church for years! Because there were nearly one hundred people who were going to be removed, each name had to be discussed, and this took up hours and hours of time. The pastor finally gave up in frustration and dropped the whole idea, though the board had in principle agreed to the change. But the reality of erasing from the church rolls those whom they had known years before was just too much; they kept bringing up endless hypothetical situations: What would their family think if we did this? Should we contact them one last time? Once you have made a decision regarding your church's ministry, if you cave due to pressure from individuals, you might find the next thing that you want to do in your church to be impossible.

5.  *The Pastor and the Board: Part Three.* Some boards have a member or members who want to be the real leader of the church, despite the fact that the church looks to the pastor to fulfill that role. The board member does not want to do the pastor's job but does want to make the decisions that will determine how the church will function, what programs it will offer, how it will spend its money, and perhaps even run the staff, as well. The motives that guide this type of person can vary from thinking that he is the smartest and most knowledgeable about the church to a simple desire for power over others. How the church is structured might affect the ability for board members to control the pastor and have more influence than is proper. If a church requires a chairman and gives broad powers to this person, the pastor can become an employee subservient to the board. If someone other than the

pastor brings the agenda to the board meetings, the pastor's concerns might not even be discussed by the board.

If there is a board member who is trying to control the church through his position, the pastor has some options to try and correct this situation. There can be fewer meetings. Some members will welcome this; the pastor can offer this as a way for them to spend more time with their families, doing ministry, etc. The pastor can try and make this board member his friend and confidant so that he can dilute his control by becoming his advisor. The pastor might confide to another board member that he trusts (I hope you trust all of your board members, but we are dealing with the real world here) and see if he agrees that the board member the pastor has concerns about is behaving badly and get their opinion on how they would handle the situation. The pastor may have to bring this up in a board meeting and see what happens, with the ultimate result that he may have to replace that board member, either by voting him off the board (if he has the votes) or by asking him to step down or not run again when the term is up. Lastly, the pastor may approach the board member privately and honestly share his concerns about the man's behavior, though I think it is better if this is done with another person, preferably another board member. There is less room for misunderstanding if another person is involved. A church can only have one leader; the pastor was given that role when he was called by the church. I will offer this caveat: if a pastor is not leading the church, someone else will. If the pastor has not fulfilled the role of leader and has let others take this role, it is extremely difficult to get it back.

Whatever you decide, do not let this go on forever. The longer this goes on, the harder it will be to resolve; people usually become entrenched in their bad behavior.

6. *Professional Christians.* People in our culture many times find much of their identity from what they do. This should not

surprise us; work takes up much of our time, energy, and talents. As Christians, our main identity should come from being God's beloved children, not from our occupation, whatever that may be. If you are a pastor, you can fall prey to this temptation; you can view your occupation as pastor as something special, something privileged, a higher calling than your congregation, and you can become what I call a "professional Christian." It is true that your education, your position, and your gifts set you apart from those you lead and minister to, but God help you if you allow these circumstances to make you proud, superior, or elevated from those you serve. Because you usually know more about the Bible, tell others what it means, deal with their problems, and have authority and leadership that others do not have, you will be tempted to think yourself better and more spiritual than your congregation. You can avoid this by following these principles.

a. Remind yourself of all the mistakes you have made in your ministry.

b. Remind yourself of all your weaknesses and times you have given in to temptation.

c. Remind yourself that though you are to lead your church, you are also to serve in humility.

d. Remind yourself that your family knows what you are really like.

e. Remind yourself that your education is just that, an education, not a special dispensation that makes you better than your congregation.

f. Remind yourself of what others go through in their jobs by meeting with those who are not pastors. You will find many men find too much of their identity in the work, to the detriment of their families and their walk with God.

7. *The Pastor and the Board: Part Four.* Many board members who serve in Evangelical churches have never read a book on theology, church renewal, church history, church and culture, relevant issues (emerging church, for example), and show little curiosity about these things. A pastor can help them as elders by suggesting books they can read, bringing up issues in the Evangelical world that are of concern to him, and holding them accountable to broadening their knowledge of all things biblical. Many elders/board members feel that it is the pastor's responsibility to know these things; they are to be concerned with their specific church and its ministry. A pastor may or may not be able to do this with every member of the board, but it is likely that some will respond to his leadership in this area. This, of course, assumes that the pastor is a reader and has at least some understanding of what is going on in the church world at large.

   Another responsibility that the board should have is to make sure that the pastor is doing well spiritually. This will happen if the board spends time dealing with each other on a personal level and discusses things other than just church business. Still, a pastor must let others ask him about his life. It just won't automatically happen, and it would be better if someone other than the pastor led this part of the meeting.

8. *Dealing with disappointment.* Every job has its disappointments. Because we live in a broken world, disappointment is common. Disappointment can be defined as being frustrated, let down, disenchanted, or disillusioned. It often relates to not meeting the expectations you have regarding whatever is causing your disappointment. If your marriage is not meeting your expectations, disappointment can set in. If your expectations concerning your ministry as pastor are not being met, again,

disappointment can set in. If not dealt with, disappointment can lead to stress, hurt, and depression. There are other areas of life where you will no doubt suffer disappointment, but it can be difficult to deal with the disappointment that comes from difficulties in the pastorate. There are several ways you will experience disappointment as a pastor.

a.  Your church has not grown as much as you (or your board/congregation) thought it would.

b.  Your messages are not being hailed as the greatest thing since sliced bread.

c.  Your board is causing you stress and anxiety.

d.  Your family is showing signs of weariness or resignation at your involvement in the ministry.

e.  Your finances are tight while others in your church live in large homes and drive new cars.

f.  You cannot seem to get ahead of the personal problems your church members continually bring to you.

It is easy to write that God is bigger than your disappointments, but it is nonetheless true. If you expected to go into the pastorate and not have times of discouragement and disappointment specifically related to your work, your Bible college, seminary, or other pastors failed you miserably. If you are convinced that you are in the place that God wants you, then He can help you find a measure of joy and satisfaction in what you do, despite all of the things that might conspire to rob you of that joy. The devil knows that if he can bring a pastor down through sin or discouragement, the church that he pastors will for a time lose much of its effectiveness. The worst thing that you can do is to suffer in silence; find someone you trust that you can talk to, whether in or out of your church (there is nothing wrong with your board knowing that there are times when you feel disenchanted with your job). I would suggest that your wife is sometimes not the best person to unload your disappointment on; she has enough to occupy her thoughts and life.

9.  *Why pastors burn out.* Pastors aren't the only people who burn out at their jobs. By burn out, I am thinking of working too many hours, physical exhaustion, nervousness, anxiety, and dreading going to work each day. Burnout usually results in the loss of a job, whether it is in the ministry or the secular world. There is a progression to a person burning out at their job; it does not happen all at once. Here are some signs that signal you may be headed for burnout.

    a.  **Pastors work too many hours.** If a pastor works more than fifty hours a week for extended periods of time, he may be headed for a fall. Some men say they work sixty or seventy hours a week, but unless they are robbing themselves of sleep, this will be about all they do with their lives. Who wants to live like that? Because a pastor's job involves dealing continually with people he has a personal investment in, the hours he works can take more out of him emotionally and physically than other types of employment. If he is not getting any exercise, does not have a hobby, is depriving himself of sleep, or is overweight from eating too much or the wrong things, then he is a candidate for pastoral burnout. These things are signs of a life that is out of balance.

    b.  **Pastors are doing things in the church that other people should be trained to do.** The pastor has to preach the message (though there is nothing that says he has to preach every week). If he has those in the church who are gifted speakers, let them preach once in a while, not just when the pastor is on vacation. The pastor will do most of the counseling (though he can get others involved in this if they are qualified), and he will do most of the visiting (elders can help in this ministry, as well). If he makes it a priority to train others in the church to do things that are causing him to work too many hours and he lets the congregation know that this is how he will help people use their gifts and talents, he can ease his burden and get some of his life back. After preaching, one of the pastor's main functions should be to train others to do ministry, freeing him from the burden of carrying the church on his back (see Eph. 4:11, 12).

c. **The pastor's spiritual life is dry and barren,** and he feels that he has nothing to give to the church. Because he is the leader and shepherd of the church and is responsible to help the members grow in their faith, if his relationship to Christ is not vital and growing, he may feel like a hypocrite in carrying out his duties. If this persists over time, he may feel a need to leave the ministry. There are a couple of things that need to be said about burnout related to spiritual dryness. Everyone goes through times of dryness in their spiritual life; nearly every biography of Christian leaders through the centuries shows us that they all have times in their lives when their faith was weak. There is a difference between these occurrences and the barrenness that results from overwork, unmet expectations, personal problems (perhaps family or spousal), or difficulties at the church. I have known more than a few pastors who left the ministry because they just could not find the energy, motivation, or desire to do the work. Some returned after a time away from ministry; some never returned.

If you feel you are headed toward burnout, there are some things you need to do. Talk to your board, let them know how you are doing spiritually, and ask for their advice on how you should proceed. This will only work if your board is generally supportive and has an understanding of how demanding your position can be. If you feel you cannot talk to your board, find another pastor you trust and talk to him. Odds are they have felt the way you have and may be able to offer help based on their experience. It may be that you can develop a relationship with another pastor that will help take the pressure off you just by being able to talk to someone else about what you are experiencing.

If you do talk to your board, they may give you time off to renew yourself, they may have you seek professional help, or they may not understand your dilemma and/or offer advice that is not helpful or timely. Ask your family how they think you are doing, and ask them to be candid (usually this won't be a problem!) about what they think you should do. Better to leave the ministry for a time to save your family and possibly yourself than to continue in the pastorate until you have to leave because you cannot continue to do the job any longer. Some of you may consider it a sign of weakness to walk away from your church because you are physically or emotionally unable to do the work; that may be either your pride or the devil talking. Just remember, you are not going to do your church any good if you flame out in front of their eyes.

10. *The Internet.* You know what I am talking about here. I am talking about the statistics that say that up to forty percent of you will sometime this year view pornography on the Internet. There has been much written on this subject (there has been much written about pastors who have affairs, but that does not seem to have slowed the number of pastors who fall into sexual sin). There are websites dedicated to helping those of you who are caught in this type of sin. There are Internet filters available to keep you from this type of temptation, and most importantly, you know this type of behavior is wrong. If

you have been tempted in this area or are currently engaged in looking at images that shame and disgust you when you are honest with yourself, you can stop if you want. God is bigger than your lust, and you can find forgiveness and healing from this type of behavior. But you have to stop, and you have to stop today.

Find someone you trust, preferably another pastor and not someone on your board (that will come later), and tell them what you have done. This may be the hardest thing you have ever attempted, but you need to have someone who can help you control this part of your life, someone who will not judge or condemn you but work with you to become sexually pure again. Depending on how far down this road you have gone, you may have to tell your wife, as well. You will need to get the counsel of others to decide when and how to do this, but this sin has no doubt affected your relationship with your wife; you will need to ask for her forgiveness and help to regain what you have lost. Eventually, you will have to be honest with your board about your behavior; depending on how they view what you have done, you may have to leave your church. You may not feel like you have to tell them, especially if you stop the practice and gain a measure of victory; this will be your decision, but do not make this decision on your own. Get the advice and counsel of those you trust. In talking with pastors about this problem, I have found that there are certain times and circumstances that can lead men to search out websites on the Internet they have no business visiting:

1. Those of you who are prone to discouragement may look for relief in pornography. I know this does not seem to make any sense (sin seldom makes any sense), but it is nevertheless a common circumstance for those who engage in this behavior.

2. The idea that you will not get caught because of the supposed anonymity of the Internet leads some of you into this type of sin. Some of you may have had this problem for months or

years and have yet to be discovered. May I remind you that Jesus sits at your side when you view these images. You have already been discovered, and my guess is that you know it.

3.  The idea that you can stop at any time makes this behavior seem less sinful than it really is, and that it is not really controlling you in any real sense. If that is true, then stop right now.

4.  The fact that this is a "victimless" sin can somehow convince you that though it is wrong; it is no worse than any number of other sins that you or others commit. The reality is, of course, that this is not a victimless sin; you, your family, and your church are all victims, and the shame and guilt you feel reinforce this truth.

5.  Those of you who work long hours and become emotionally and physically drained from constantly giving of yourself to others seem to be in greater danger of this than those of you who have a more balanced and normal life.

6.  Finally, if your relationship with your wife is not meeting your expectations in the area of sex, you may somehow justify viewing other women as something you deserve. I know this sounds twisted, but men have been justifying similar behavior ("My wife does not understand or meet my needs, so I have to have an affair with the church secretary") since forever. If your relationship with your wife is not doing well, talk to her. Get a professional involved if you need to, but make this a priority in your life, and get back on the road to marital sanity and fulfillment.

    Finally, one last question. If you are involved in using the Internet in an inappropriate manner (that's as nice as I can say it), how do you stand up in the pulpit each Sunday and tell your people how to live and be obedient to God?

# Questions to Ponder

## Members with Money

1. Do you feel differently toward those who are rich in your church? Is this a good, bad or neutral feeling?

2. Have you personally benefited from those who have money in your church? How did that make you feel? What did they do for you? Was your wife aware of this as well? How did this affect her? Did you feel the help came with strings attached?

3. Does your church generally look with favor on those who are rich? Does your church allow rich members to give money specifically for projects that matter to them, say, a new air conditioner for the youth room?

4. Does your church rely on the giving of rich people to meet its budget, or to put it another way, do rich people in your church give a high percentage of the budget? (It may be that you do not know; in many churches the pastor does not know who gives but probably has an idea.) Does this fact bother you?

5. Have you ever been tempted to speak or act in a way that you know would have the approval of people in your church who are rich? If so, how did this make you feel?

6. As a pastor who probably makes a modest income, are you envious of the rich and how they are able to live? Has God been able to help you be content with your income? If not, why not?

## Thoughts on Sermons

1. Do you believe your sermons can affect the lives of those you speak to each week? Have you seen concrete evidence of this?

2.  What do you expect to accomplish when you preach each week? How do measure the results of your expectations?

3.  Would you preach a sermon Sunday morning if you spent the drive to church in a rage because your teenage son did not come home that night?

4.  What does your board think of your messages? Do you ever ask them?

5.  How do your messages set the tone for your church?

6.  Would your church know what your vision is for the church based on what they hear from you each week?

7.  Have you ever wept during a message? Why do you think I might ask this?

## Talking About Jesus in Church

1.  Why do you think your church members have difficulty talking about Jesus?

2.  Do you bring Jesus into your casual conversation with church members?

3.  When your congregation talks to you after the service, do you try to steer the conversation to Jesus or just go with the flow?

4.  Is talking about your sermon the same as talking about Jesus?

5.  If someone in your church said, "Pastor, tell me about Jesus," how would you respond?

6.  What can you do as pastor to make your church a more Jesus-friendly place?

## Leading through Change

1.  What experience have you had leading a church through big changes? What were these changes?

2.  On a scale of 1 to 10, how easy was this change to accomplish? What would you do differently to make the process easier?

3.  How did you use your authority and leadership as pastor to accomplish change?

4.  How well equipped are you emotionally to stand your ground once you have decided to bring change to your church?

5.  How have people tried to influence you or bring pressure on you to change your mind regarding a decision you have made in your role as pastor?

## The Pastor and the Board, Part Three

1.  Have you had board members who wanted to be the real power in the church? How did you deal with that difficulty?

2.  Why do you think some board members want the power but not the position of pastor?

3.  Have you tried to make your board a team? Has this been successful? Would you want your board to act as a team, or would this make you uncomfortable?

4.  Do you have any board members who are your friends as well? Is this possible in your current situation? How might you make a board member your friend, and how could this help your relationship to the group?

5.  Have you ever had to replace a board member? How did that go? What did you learn?

## Professional Christians

1. How much of your identity comes from your role as pastor? What would happen if you had to leave the ministry for a time and work in the "real" world? Would this make you feel less important?

2. How do you balance the two realities of being a leader and being a servant?

3. Do you view your job as pastor as something special, something that sets you apart from other Christians? If so, has this made you proud?

4. When you are with other pastors, does your conversation tend to reinforce the idea that you are in an exclusive club? Do you have an us/them mentality regarding your congregation? How might this attitude show itself?

5. Did your education give you the idea that your position as pastor sets you apart from other Christians? If so, do you believe this? If not, have you developed this attitude as you have been in ministry?

6. Do you insist that your congregation call you "pastor"? Would you mind it if they called you by your first name? Does calling you "pastor" have any negative implications regarding the issue of your personal identity? Does it have any positive implications?

## The Pastor and the Board, Part Four

1. Do you try and broaden the biblical and theological understanding of your board? If so, have you been successful? If not, why not?

2. Does your board feel that it is their responsibility to care for you spiritually? If so, what have they done to accomplish this? If not, do you think this should be part of their role as elder/board member?

3. Does your board spend time praying together? Does your board spend time dealing with personal issues of life? Is there accountability on the board for how each member is doing spiritually?

## Dealing with Disappointment

1. Has there been a time when you wanted to quit the ministry? What was the occasion? If you did not quit, what kept you from leaving?

2. On a scale of 1 to 10, how well have the expectations you had regarding the ministry been fulfilled? How realistic do you think your expectations were? Have you experienced disappointment in your role as pastor that can be traced to the job not meeting your expectations?

3. If you have suffered disappointment, has it led to something worse such as anxiety, worry, or depression? If so, how have you dealt with these emotions and feelings? Did you share how you have felt with your board? How did they respond? Were they able to offer help?

4. How did God help you get through times of disappointment? What did you learn about God during that time?

5. Was your disappointment visible to your family? How did they react? Were they able to help you?

6. Do you have someone you trust that you can go to when you experience feelings of disappointment regarding the ministry?

## Burnout

1. How close have you come to leaving the ministry due to burnout? Did anyone know at the time? If so, what did they tell you about your situation? If not, was there a reason no one knew?

2. If you are working more than fifty hours a week, how well are you holding up physically and emotionally? How is your family holding up if you are working long hours?

3. Do you consistently miss times with your family/wife because of your schedule? If so, does your board know you are missing these times? Do they care?

4. How many times in a year do you preach sermons when you feel you should be at home watching football because you are dry and barren in your spiritual life? Have you ever communicated this to your board? What would they say?

5. If you thought you were headed down the path toward burning out of the ministry, what would you do? Who would you talk to?

6. What would God think if you quit the ministry due to being overwhelmed and overworked? Do you think He would be able to help you if you were going in this direction? What could He do that would help you in that type of situation? Have you experienced His help in times like this?

7. Do you think that taking time off from the ministry is an option if you cannot seem to find the motivation, energy, or desire to continue as a pastor? How would this decision affect you personally? Your family? Your view of the ministry?

# The Internet

1. On a scale of 1 to 10, what has been your involvement in viewing inappropriate images on the Internet?

2. If you have had a problem in this area, how has it made you feel? If not, why do you think you have been able to stay away from this temptation?

3. Do you feel qualified to help other pastors who may have become ensnared in this type of sin? How would you specifically help someone who came to you and confessed to this sin?

4. How has your church addressed this issue with the men in your congregation? Have you talked about this issue with your board? Are you certain that none of your board members have a problem in this area?

5. If you are currently involved in Internet pornography, who can you call or talk to today to begin the process of confession and restoration? Will you do this?

# Conclusion

The journey through all of these churches and all of the experiences, people, and circumstances have left me with some conclusions about the church, some good and some not so good. *If you are not a pastor, these words are especially for you:*

1.  Christians need to go to church. It is not only a command; it is really the only practical way to develop relationships with other believers. What type of church you go to is your business, but if you live in the United States, the odds are that you will attend a church similar to ones that I have written about. If you are going to go, you might as well get involved on some level; if you just want to listen to a sermon every week and sings some songs, stay and home and watch a Christian TV program.

2.  If you attend church, you had better realize that churches are full of sinners just like you. Church members are going to say and do things that you will not like or appreciate; you might even get your feelings hurt. You can leave (if the situation warrants it), like I did, or you might try and work things out. Jesus Himself knew that churches would be places where people would say and do things to each other that would cause problems; the only time He really talked about the church in the gospels was to address these types of issues (Mt. 18:15-20).

3.  The most important reality of any church is its leadership, including both the pastor and the board. These men set the structure, philosophy, expectations, and goals of the church. The pastor, for good or bad, will always be the face of the church and will be the one on whom success (in a professional

manner—I am not discounting God) will ultimately depend. If he has a vision, can implement that vision through ministries and other strategies, has the backing of the board, and does not let the fact that he is in charge go to his head, as it were, then the odds are that the church will do well. In my view, the pastor should be the visionary, the man who is responsible for training lay people to do the bulk of the ministry and who can bring about change if it is needed because he has the power of the pulpit and the position of leader.

4. Finally, church is only a place to worship, fellowship, learn, and reach out to the others. We should never derive our identity or meaning from what we do at church, or it will become an idol. Our meaning and identity come from God, to Him be the glory.

# Epilogue

If you Google the phrases "pastor burnout," "pastor statistics" or "pastor surveys," you will find the following startling information from various websites. From my experience, most congregations have no idea that things are so bad out there; they only know their own situation. Pastors and those who study churches, however, know the truth: that the job of pastor is not for the faint of heart.

*Fifteen hundred pastors leave the ministry each month due to moral failure, burnout, or contention in their churches.*

One pastor I know has kept a list for about twenty years now that includes the names of those who have left the ministry due to "moral failure" (sexual sin). This list currently has over two hundred names on it. In my ministry with pastors, most have difficulty in two areas: money and sex.

Pastor, what are you doing to keep yourself morally pure? How is your relationship with your wife? If you have drifted apart, either emotionally or physically, you might be setting yourself up for a fall in this area.

*Fifty percent of pastor's marriages will end in divorce.* Taking into account all of these statistics, I am surprised the number isn't higher, aren't you? Some doubt that this number is quite this high; some surveys say 38 percent, but still, these are men whom we look to as leaders of our churches. There is no doubt that it is primarily their occupation as pastor that leads to a percentage of divorce that is this high.

Pastor, if I asked your wife what the odds were that your marriage would end in divorce, how would she answer? If I asked her a year from now, what would she say? Have you had friends in the ministry whose marriages have ended in divorce? Do you know why? Are there lessons for you from these tragedies?

*Fifty percent of pastors are so discouraged that they would leave the ministry if they could but have no other way to make a living.*

What does a pastor put on his resume? I talk to people for an hour a week from an elevated position. I listened to people's problems, but they would not let me solve them. My college training equipped me to know everything about the Bible. I coordinate groups of volunteers to do a bunch of tasks that are unique to a church. I am not allowed to handle money. I can't make decisions on my own, etc. etc. etc. Is it any wonder that most pastors feel that they are not qualified to do any other type of work?

Pastor, if you want to leave the ministry, it is no disgrace. Better to save your family and your life than to continue on as a pastor because you feel it is your calling and duty. God has promised He will provide for your needs; you will be able to find another source of employment and ministry.

*Eighty percent of seminary and Bible school graduates who enter the ministry will leave within the first five years. Ninety percent of pastors said their seminary or Bible training did only a fair to poor job preparing them for ministry.* Why do they leave? Because the reality they find in the churches they minister in usually does not match their expectations, and when they find they cannot accomplish what they set out to do, many throw in the towel and leave the ministry altogether. As for seminary not training pastors for the reality they find in churches, the actual percentage is probably closer to 100 percent, but 10 percent apparently do not want to admit they spent all of that time and money for nothing.

Pastor, your expectations of what you will experience in the ministry will largely determine your success. If your expectations are based in reality, you might survive more than five years; if not, good luck, but realize you will probably be included in this statistic. For a reality check, find a pastor you do not know personally and ask him about his time as a pastor, preferably one who has been in the ministry for more than five years.

*Seventy percent of pastors feel grossly underpaid.* Here's a thought: make the pastor's salary the average of his board. One of two things will happen: the pastor will either get a pay raise or the church will get a new board that makes less money.

Pastor, if you feel you are underpaid, how is this affecting your ministry? Does your board know how you feel? If you are underpaid, have you asked your board for a raise?

*Ninety percent said the ministry was completely different than what they thought it would be before they entered the ministry.* This is largely the blame of seminaries and Bible colleges. Because they are not based in the real world of churches, they do not prepare pastors for what they will face. Or they just don't want to tell them; perhaps they think if they tell the truth no one will want to go in the ministry in the first place and these institutions would disappear.

Seminary students and pastors in waiting, again, talk to someone who has been a pastor of a church that would be similar to what you might pastor, and find out how churches really work.

*Eighty percent of pastors' wives feel their spouse is overworked.* If a pastor does not make it a priority to train lay people (or his board) to do the ministry of the church, he will end up doing most everything or feel like he needs to do everything because he is the only one who knows how. Many pastors' wives jump every time the phone rings, knowing that it is probably someone who needs her husband right that second. Who wants to live like that?

Pastor, if your wife feels this way, what are you doing to work a normal amount of hours? If you are afraid to cut back your hours for fear of what the board or the church will think, it's time to look for another church or perhaps another type of work. If you choose your ministry over your family, you will probably lose them both.

*Eighty percent of pastors' wives wish their spouse would choose another profession.* What, and give up your "calling"? The sad reality is that the things that you learn in seminary are not readily transferable to other careers, and what guy wants to admit he made a giant mistake or that perhaps God did not call him to the ministry? Pastors' wives look at the normalcy of other people's schedules and are jealous that many of their friends and neighbors do not take their jobs home with them and are not at the beck and call of dozens or hundreds of people.

Pastor, if your wife cannot find fulfillment or happiness with you in the ministry, and there is no hope of that changing, your relationship to her is more important than your role as a pastor. Honor your wife by realizing some women are just not cut out to be the wife of a pastor; there is more to life than "full-time" ministry. Indeed, many pastors who leave the ministry for secular employment find fulfillment and opportunity in their new position and other ways to minister that use their gifts and abilities.

*The majority of pastors' wives surveyed said that the most destructive event that has occurred in their marriage and family was the day they entered the ministry.* In what other job are you literally on call 24/7, can be fired without notice (in most cases), do not have a human resource department to fight for you rights as an employee, seldom get a pension, and usually have inadequate benefits (most pastors are self-employed, and so they buy their benefits; some get by with no benefits or use the benefits provided by the spouse's work, if she is employed), constantly have people telling you how to do your job or how to do it better, have to live up to unrealistic expectations, and because the people who "work" for you (the congregation and the board) are not paid, you have no real power to get them to do anything nor are they accountable to you like they would be in a business environment? *Enough said.*

*Seventy percent of pastors constantly fight depression.* Does this surprise any of us? So when your pastor is in the pulpit preaching each Sunday, on at least some of those mornings the last thing that he feels like doing is telling you how to live your life.

Pastor, don't suffer in silence. Find someone you can share your depression with; another pastor will certainly know what you are going through. It may be that you will need to talk to a professional; there are Christian counselors who have experience in helping pastors through difficult times in the ministry. Just because you are a pastor does not mean you are not prone to times of discouragement and difficulty; in fact, it is more likely that you will suffer emotional distress in the ministry because of the demands it places on you and your family.

*Almost forty percent surveyed said they have had an extramarital affair since beginning their ministry.* That's forty percent who would admit it. How many pastors do you think are still in the ministry hiding the fact that they are adulterers? Imagine the guilt and shame they are living with each and every day. Pastors have unique temptations in their work setting; vulnerable people come to them on a regular basis seeking help for problems that often include dissatisfaction with their spouses. My pastor will not counsel women without having either his wife or another woman present and many times will refer a lady to a professional woman counselor. And it is not just pastors; two of my Bible college professors lost their wives to other men who were not as busy as they were in doing God's work. My father-in-law once told me that absence makes the heart grow fonder...of someone else.

Pastor, these affairs usually do not happen spontaneously, though it does occur occasionally. You know in your heart if you are becoming emotionally attached to another woman or drifting away from your wife. Other women may look up to you as a pastor and someone who can provide for them something their husbands cannot, and so they become attracted to you. Frequently, pastors get involved with women they see at church or who work as staff. I never allow myself to have a conversation alone with a woman that lasts more than a few minutes; I always find a way to disengage myself. Maybe I am paranoid, but I have known too many men who have fallen into sexual sin who I never thought would succumb to that type of temptation. You may think that you would never engage in any type of sexual sin. I am sure there are thousands of other pastors who thought that as well and are now out of the ministry and have ruined their families. If your marriage is not what you want it to be, talk to your wife honestly and get help if you need to. Please do not destroy yourself, your family, or your church by getting involved with another woman; you will regret it for the rest of your life.

*Seventy percent of pastors do not have a close friend, confidant, or mentor.*

Who wants to be the friend of somebody with these kinds of statistics? That's unfair, but you get the point. Church boards should make it a priority to make sure that the pastor has the opportunity to develop relationships with other men in the church. One pastor I know has been in an accountability group with men in his church for a number of years, a practice that has allowed him to participate and grow with them in different areas of life.

Pastor, if you do not have a close friend you can hang out with, find one. You need to do things with other men that are not church related—fishing, golfing, or even meeting for lunch on occasion will help take some of your energy and focus away from church, which will help balance your life out. Share this desire with your board, and have them hold you accountable to develop this type of relationship. If you do not have someone you can talk with about your life (in addition to your wife, who should not be burdened with everything church or work related), your perspective will be limited to your role as pastor.

*One hundred percent of pastors had a close associate or seminary friend who had left the ministry because of burnout, conflict in their church, or moral failure.* Yet most men think that this will not happen to them—they are smarter, more spiritual, more faithful, more committed than those who could not make it in the ministry.

Pastor, what steps are you taking to make sure you do not become included in this statistic?

*Eighty-one percent of pastors in one survey said that their church had no regular discipleship program or effective way to deepen the lives of their members.* Most of the pastor's time is spent running programs that only maintain the status quo; few pastors have developed programs to train their own congregations to do the work of the church. Similarly, few pastors know how to train leaders of small groups in how to use those groups to move their members along in their spiritual journey. Since most churches have less than 50 percent of their adult congregation in small groups, I guess it doesn't really matter that there are no trained leaders, does it?

Pastor, this relates specifically to your church's small group ministry. If you have small groups, are they accomplishing the task of maturing your congregation in the faith? If you don't have small groups or you feel they are not meeting your expectations, make this a priority in your ministry until you succeed.

*Seventy-two percent of pastors state that they only study the Bible when they have to prepare sermons.* Who is it who is helping the pastor in being sure he is spiritually healthy? Most congregations and church boards assume that the pastor is doing fine so they never ask him about his life. We have already discovered that the pastor has few friends. It's like he is hung out there (wherever "there" is) to twist in the wind alone.

Pastor, how do you approach the Bible? You have to study it somewhat academically to prepare your messages, but if you find you cannot read the Bible devotionally, looking for what God wants to communicate to you, ask God to forgive you for letting your heart become hard toward His Word. It might help you to read the Bible on your knees, praying as you read for a fresh word from Him for your spirit.

*Ninety percent of pastors are worn out or fatigued.* Ever seen a hamster in a cage running endlessly on a wheel and getting nowhere? *Enough said.*

*Pastors report that only 25 percent of church members attend a Bible study group at least two times a month.* If it is true that most spiritual growth occurs in the context of small groups, then most of the people who attend evangelical churches are not growing and no doubt feel a sense of dissatisfaction in their Christian lives. This is what Willow Creek Church in Chicago, Illinois, found out when they surveyed their congregation. You can order the book they wrote from this survey called *Reveal*; you can find it at their website, www.

Willowcreek.org. (It is worth noting that Willow Creek developed a conference based on their survey also called *Reveal*. I guess it takes some real confidence to have a conference based on what you did wrong and how your church was not growing spiritually.)

Pastor, you cannot get your congregation involved in small groups if you do not have them. If you do have them up and running, there are ways to promote and encourage your members to attend. You must insist that your leaders/board members attend a small group to set an example. If they don't, why would your members? You might also consider clearing out your church's schedule for a time so everyone has the ability to fit attendance at a small group into their busy schedules. Small groups are usually the only place your congregation can fulfill their obligation to care and relate to each other, so get on it!

*In one survey taken of pastors, 78 percent reported that they were forced to resign at least once, and 63 percent were fired at least twice.*

How much notice do you think these men received from their church boards, and how many do you think saw it coming? Why were they fired or forced to resign?

1.  Fifty-two percent said it was over organizational or control issues. My guess is that this involved the boards that they served with. Somebody did not get their way, and guess who lost the battle of wills?

2.  Twenty-four percent said that there was a conflict that they as pastor could not resolve. Who wants to work in an environment where you cannot ever get a moment of peace? In a similar fashion,

3.  Fourteen percent said there was resistance to their leadership. Some of this may be the fault of the pastor. He may not be a good leader, he may not communicate what he is trying to accomplish, but most of the time I suspect that there are

other issues (such as control, personality, or fear of change) that are at work here.

Pastor, if you have been forced to leave a church, it is not the end of the world. God will have other opportunities for you to minister; the question is how being forced to leave a church will affect your view of the church and your role as pastor. Being forced to leave a church many times becomes inevitable because of the way you entered the church—not knowing the church dynamics, not knowing the real leaders, not knowing the history, not talking to the former pastor, etc. The more you know going in, the longer you may last in that church, so don't be afraid to ask every question you can think of, and be honest in your answers to what you are asked by those who are interviewing you.

*Are you a member of an Evangelical church?* This is your pastor we are talking about, and in all likelihood, no matter what he looks like or how he behaves on the surface, some of these things will be true of him. Can I give you some advice? Give him a break! You have in your power the ability to make his life more satisfying and his ministry more productive by doing a few simple things:

Be encouraging; say something positive to him, and not just about his sermons. Tell him you pray for him regularly. If you are a lady, take his wife out to lunch. If you are a guy, take the pastor out to lunch, but don't talk about church. If you have concerns about the church, why not ask somebody on the board and tell them not to bother the pastor about it, but have them tell you what is going on about this or that. If someone is being negative about the pastor, stop and say, "Let's pray for him right now. He has such a hard job. He needs our prayers for wisdom, grace, and strength." Ask him what new things he has planned for the church, and for God's sake (and the sake of the church He uses to accomplish His work), be open to new things. Ask a board member how the pastor is doing. Are they taking care of him? Is he working too hard? Is he discouraged? Let them know you are counting on them to support the pastor and make sure he is not overworked or underpaid. It is congregations and boards that have the ability to control the pastor's workplace experience. It takes deliberate effort to make sure the pastor has the atmosphere and conditions to do his job effectively.

Finally,

*Eighty-five percent of pastors said their greatest problem is they are sick and tired of dealing with problem people such as elders, deacons, worship leaders, worship teams, board members, and associate pastors.* This is you, people! Some of this may be the fact that the pastor is a lousy leader, he has no vision, he is incompetent, or he cannot get along with people, etc. But if we are honest, church congregations and boards are usually (from what I have observed not only as a church member and board member but as a trainer of pastors who has listened to their stories, stories that have left me in tears) the cause of much of these statistics that have been cited above. I suspect that because of the way pastors are trained and the how they arrive in churches via the resume system, these circumstances contribute to these frightful numbers and I have no expectation that they will change any time soon. That just means that it is up to individual churches to treat their ministers with the respect and dignity they deserve as servants of Christ and not drive them out of the ministry altogether.

Pastor, you will just not be able to change how some people act or what they will say that will affect your ministry in the church you pastor. You have to be able to rise above those who are immature, hurtful, resistant to your leadership, and generally difficult to work with. Every church has people like this. If you ask God for the grace and strength to help you lead those who are difficult, He will do this, though He may not change the hearts and minds of those you lead at the time of your choosing.